Tiger Mountain
Hispanics in the Vietnam War

Tiger Mountain
Hispanics in the Vietnam War

By
Z. E. Sanchez

ISBN 978-1-300-36032-2

In Memory of
All Hispanic Vietnam Veterans
And Their Buddies

Contents

viii

Introduction to Tiger Mountain

The long shadow of the Vietnam War bends with the times, casting in stark relief those who were there, regardless of race, creed or wealth. For those who had access to media coverage, their stories were told a long time ago. The eventual welcome home parades, a decade late, helped to heal the initial rejection that many veterans experienced. But there are still those whose stories remain to be told.

This is an account in their own words by Hispanic soldiers, marines and airmen of their intense, demanding, heroic and traumatic years in the Vietnam War. There is no cross-referencing of information: These men will stand or fall by their individual stories, by the authenticity of what they are telling us. It's not a true story: It is *their* story.

I found the men living in the Northwestern states of Washington, Oregon and Idaho. Several of the men may have been born in either Texas or somewhere in the Southwest, but their formative years were spent in the high plains of the North. One of the men, Don Neptune, is not Hispanic, but also from the Northwest. I found Don like I found the other men, by word of mouth. Each veteran I interviewed seemed to point to another veteran. Relatives or friends who knew them also pointed them out. I did not go about my search in a pre-determined manner; rather, I was like an explorer who kept being pointed to something just beyond the horizon.

The men were still relatively young when I interviewed them. What they say about their rite of passage as ordinary American soldiers is as varied as their personalities. These interviews took place only a decade or so after the end of the war. Who they were as young men, what they saw and experienced "before" Vietnam made them the soldiers they became.

Sergio Armijo, ex-Special Forces, recounts how he was "pushed" out into the world of white people through his army experiences. Before the army he had never lived among whites. In Vietnam he learned that all men cry and scream in terror equally, regardless of color. Simon Carranza, an MP (Military Police), makes little or no reference to being Hispanic while in Vietnam; it is only after his return when he applies for a police officer's job that it becomes an issue. Some men are more willing, or able, than others to penetrate to the small differences that make a Hispanic soldier Hispanic.

Several of the men returned to have successful careers after Vietnam. Just a few examples: Green Beret Sergio Armijo became a Superior Court judge in Seattle; the Marine Corp's Lionel Guerra, wounded on an engagement called Hill 881 North, became a bank vice-president in his community; and ex-Army Captain Robert Sanchez operated his own small martial arts studio for many years, and watched his own son become an elite Army Ranger and a lieutenant colonel.

The Air Force's Antonio Santoy strongly retained a sense of who he was culturally and spoke about it compassionately and with insight. He treasured his service with his fellow airmen, regardless of color. After Vietnam, Tony became a state employee, sacrificing long hours of his own time as a community planner. Though not in combat, he did experience mortar fire, and the deadlier exposure to the chemical defoliant, Agent Orange. He died from the cancerous effects of the chemical in 1998 before he could grow old. Tony speaks with affection of the Mexican Americans, Puerto Ricans and others he met in Vietnam. He conveys a shared sense of culture that pulled these men together. The get-togethers they held resemble those of other American servicemen in movies like *Platoon*, but the choice of food (frijoles and tortillas) or music (*Little Joe y la Familia*, etc.) is different. In his narrative, Antonio points out how Chicanos from Texas and California sometimes clashed on identity issues and integration. The incidents he mentions could be instructive not only as Hispanics continue to define themselves today, but in how Hispanics and Anglos view each other.

Robert Sanchez, my older brother, was reluctant to take any hard position on the identity issue. As an enlisted man, he enjoyed the banter among blacks, whites and Hispanics. However, on arriving in Vietnam as an officer, his perspective changed.

"Vietnam was a different situation; Vietnam was a life-threatening situation," he said. "If something along those lines (racial) was said in Vietnam, it was said in a serious fashion." In Vietnam, things that were said as a joke, with regards to race or ethnic background could have serious consequences. Things changed dramatically in that environment. He discusses the difficulties of being an officer in a combat situation, but is reluctant to blame it on race. That type of thing was not easily identifiable, he says. Too many variables at play, and the responsibility was crushing.

I was still in high school when my brother, Bob, came home on leave. It had grown dark outside when Logan, a friend with the unruly long hair of the era, accompanied my brother and me across an open field between a road and a railroad track. Logan was strongly against the war. The year was probably 1965. Logan may have said something that could only come out of the mouth of a high school kid, perhaps questioning the senselessness of the war. It's been a long time: what was it that he said? Or did I say it and Logan agreed? My brother had left the field of combat only a day or two before. I couldn't see his response. It was too dark. I couldn't see his face, but I could hear the pain in his voice. There was a choking sound as he tried to respond. He said his men were normal guys who hadn't wanted to die. Friendly artillery had recently killed two of them. One of those soldiers had children he loved. I regretted deeply having been a part of his pain. A decade later when I was interviewing my brother I couldn't connect with the same emotion. Something had been lost in the intervening years.

One of the other men, Lionel Guerra, a marine, told me years later that he had been very nervous about being interviewed. He was shot in Vietnam and later qualified as 100% disabled. In 2011 when I enrolled in an online class to revisit the book, the instructor marveled that I could have gotten the men to share their experiences. I was there myself, I told her, though not as an infantryman. I spent 22 months (1969-71) in Vietnam locked in a sealed Intelligence Center, in a square, windowless, concrete building, looking at photographic evidence of bombing campaigns along the Ho Chi Minh Trail. I looked at shattered enemy transport trucks among the bomb craters. When I wasn't working, I got out into the city of Saigon, and once out into the Delta.

In the city, I did experience the shock of an explosive (called IED's in today's terms) detonated near an American PX. This was mild compared to what most of these other men experienced. In a separate incident I picked up a dead officer's belongings after he was killed by a bomb. But terrorist activities were rare while I was there; and when they did happen they happened to another soldier or civilian. That might have been enough if the veterans had asked me for details of my own experience. If they had asked I would have told them that things were mostly quiet while I was there. But I may have shared a certain tension with them, an uncertainty that stayed with me after my return home. Maybe it was through this shared tension, theirs pulled tighter than mine, mine more forgettable, that they saw it possible to share what they had seen. They gave us their stories, and allowed me record them finally.

When I think back on the interviews, I see the faces of the men, downward looking at times, inward looking, then I see them looking not at a physical distance with boundaries but a distance of years. They've already put those pictures, those memories, in a place where they will be securely stored for a long time to come. Some speak in rapid, machinegun bursts, in confused picture frames. Rudy Alaniz's first attempt to tell me about an ambush on a hill was like this. His narrative was one that I partially reconstructed because the action was so confused, and his narrative was likewise confused. I showed him the final write-up and he approved it. Earlier he had revealed a survivor's guilt, concerned that his small stature and Latino appearance spared him. I asked him whether any other Hispanics had been killed in the ambush. He said yes. I pointed out that since other Hispanics had been shot it made it unlikely that he was chosen to be spared. I never saw Rudy again, as I moved out of state; so I don't know whether the interviews made any difference in his outlook. I know he did go back to the military, using a part of my write-up of his experience. He subsequently became an officer. He had been intense, at first coming out with a jumble of impressions and images. It took me a while to form a coherent image of what had happened to him during the ambush. The narratives of the other men were at times a synthesis of the questions I asked which they confirmed, and their own discourse.

Some of the men were more reflective, slower in their ruminations than others. Some of them hardly knew me at the time, but perhaps trusted that I really was a Vietnam veteran by the tenor of my questions. I can visualize them now, each one interviewed in a different setting. Sometimes I see the motel where we met, the green trees and telephone poles in a small area. Other times I see the face of the veteran as he sits in a stiff-backed chair with a certain anticipation as to how the interview will proceed. Sometimes we are walking in a subdivision to the car, and I'm being drawn back to the subject at hand, reminded that other topics are off limits. These men were not voluble, not given to talking for talking's sake. Sergio Armijo, the Green Beret, did tell me privately that you can't make friends as an adult like the type of friends you had as a child growing up. So it occurs to me today how remarkable it was that he and the others could confide in me long enough to put their words down on paper. After the interviews, we all went on with our lives. I relocated out of the Northwest, following my 8 to 5 job across the country. At least one of the men died: Tony Santoy. Others moved from the small and large towns where I found them. Some are still there, or in the big cities. They are hard to find. Even after they are gone, their stories will be here.

Acknowledgments

In Appreciation for the Consideration of the Veterans Interviewed and their Wives for giving me their time.

Chapter One

Lightning, Ambushes, and Snakes

Rudy Alaniz
1967 68
Americal Division

"Suddenly I'm thrown through the air. Rather, I'm surprised, manhandled by some absolutely overwhelming force, some giant hand of sheer power." Rudy Alanis

From the Sky Was God
First Combat
With the Marines
Australians
Patrols
The Crater
The Lieutenant
Night
Day
Busted
Benito
The Flak Jacket
The Kill Zone
In A Cradle
From Within Me
A Second Ship
The Sky
Stateside
An Afterthought, 1985

From the Sky Was God

What tore up Rudy Alaniz was to have this guy Reynolds survive it all, up on the hill, the ambush, only to be killed in the end by a bolt of lightning.

"I used to think anything that came from the sky was God. I couldn't believe God would save his life and then kill him later. Why save his life in a kill zone where the odds were 100 to 1 and then kill him?

"God had control, I thought. I was lost, bewildered. I kept praying at night, promised myself I'd go to church if I made it.

"I lost faith in Him, but kept praying because I wanted Him on my side. Philosophically speaking, if God wants you dead, you're going to die.

"I couldn't believe God would save Reynolds' life against those odds and then kill him. Before that happened, I believed that everything that came out of the sky came from God."

First Combat

"The squad leader said, 'We were going to take that hill at such and such a time and when I tell you to move out, move out! When you see the choppers firing, where you see the tracers, that is where you fire.' We could hear the mortars and see the choppers firing the tracers as we moved up. We took turns firing, always moving with a backup and suddenly the flares went off and it was like daylight."

With the Marines

"I was with the Americal Division. We would support the Marines a lot. When they would take a hill, we would come in and replace them. But we would also do joint operations with them. Anyway, they gave me two Marines to go with me on patrol. They had their own equipment, and they knew how to lay out the claymores (mines) and the hand grenades and flares. They helped to set up the perimeter.

"I can't say that the Marines are not good fighters because I've never seen them in action, but these particular ones they gave me decided that once the perimeter was set up, they were going to take it easy. I was the squad leader, an Acting Jack, and the two Marines told me, 'We're not going to stay here 'cause it's raining like hell and we're not going to get wet. We're going to go down to that little hootch and stay there and when it's over in the morning, you come and wake us up.'

"We tried to talk 'em out of it. 'Stay here,' we told 'em. 'It's safe. We've got claymores on the main trail, trip flares, and we got the perimeter set up.'

"'Yeah,' they replied, 'it looks like you got the fort held down. You guys wake us up in the morning.'

"We didn't see them again until morning. About four or five o'clock in the morning we heard a big bang and the hootch was just totaled out."

Australians

"We backed up the Aussies. We swept the area after them. They burned down all the hootches and threw the people inside. They believed they built up respect that way. Later on we did the same thing.

"Near Hill 54, we were in the rear when the VC raided a village. One of our companies hit back and we were put on alert. When we got there they were dragging out the bodies and putting them in piles, some villagers and some NVA. We cleared out the ringleaders like this every three or so months.

"The NVA or VC would attack every three months. They would come in to kill the village leaders they didn't like and so forth. The village people would take sides and we would come in at night and clean up.

"The NVA were trying to take over and we couldn't let that happen.

"The Australians were more realistic. They would come in and wipe out the village entirely. The village was helping the NVA so they would wipe it out, hootch by hootch.

"Working like this with the Australians made it easier for the Americal to become hardened. But from our own officers we got this, 'Don't shoot them unless they have a rifle.' Only problem is that if you hesitated you got killed. Nice guys or religious guys, they didn't last. They hesitated long enough to die. I felt it at first, too. I cried at first at night.

"When I got drafted, I wanted religion. I wanted him, the priest, to say, 'Don't take another man's life.' But they didn't."

Patrols

"I was the only new guy in the unit for about six months. I was the second for about one month and then I became Point Man. Our old Point Man had been transferred, and there weren't too many guys who wanted to walk point.

"The way it works when you're walking point is that the first guy shoots quick, at random; he depends on the second and third guy to see where you are shooting and they actually get the kills.

"Adkins was my Second and he was about the best you could ask for ... Brown was Point for another platoon and he was killed as Point one month before his time was up in 'Nam.

"There were a lot of vines where we were at. I used a machete to cut a trail and wouldn't carry my rifle a lot of the times. We usually cleared our own trails except when we were in a hurry, then we'd go through old trails but that was dangerous.

"We would protect our approaches on LP (Listening Post) by straightening out the safety pins on our grenades and by putting out flares on the wire. We'd string wire and put one grenade on the path, then we'd put some twigs out there, crossed twigs. Sometimes we'd put up ration cans with rocks on 'em. There was no way the enemy was going to walk in on us undetected.

"One day we were walking, crossing a creek, and this black guy behind me got shot, right in the heart. I realized right then and there that I could have died. (The black GI didn't suffer much. He just died like that, quick.) It made the skin on my forehead crawl up and tighten up.

"In Vietnam, we lost a lot of men to the climate and to dumb accidents. You had to be careful. I had good training when I got there. Being one of the smallest men in my unit, they made me a tunnel rat. They trained me to drop a big rock in a hole before going in, to grab a branch and sweep around to set off any trip wires. Some guys would throw down a flashlight or put the flashlight at the end of a branch and the enemy would shoot at it.

"One time I went down and started crawling with the flashlight in front, holding my pistol ready. I went around this corner. I saw a bright pair of eyes and fired instantly. I waited two minutes (it seemed like a lifetime) to turn the flashlight on again. It was only a small black dog. I had been confronted with a potentially dangerous situation and I had acted correctly.

"I became the weapons squad leader. We had two M 60 machineguns with two ammo bearers per gun. The ammo bearers carried the tripod and lots of ammo in empty claymore (mine) bags. The cardboard boxes for the ammo fit okay in those bags.

"Most of the men carried their M-60 ammo Pancho Villa style wrapped around their chest and waist. It was a good way to carry extra ammo; each strap had 60 rounds.

"Another man would carry an M 79 grenade launcher. He could carry 5 to 10 rounds and his close friends would carry more ammo for him. If you liked his art you carried more M 79 rounds for him. Some guys turned their shooting into an art and other guys would respect this. One guy could put his rounds into a door at 200 meters. In woody terrain, it became difficult to use the grenade launcher so we didn't carry M-79 ammo.

"On patrol we would come across these chilitos (hot peppers) that grew wild in the mountains and valleys. We would pick these, us and the Puerto Ricans. We would raid the messhalls or Supply and get the big cans of fruit cocktail and take turns carrying these. We'd cook big meals, throw in some pork and beans and put the chilies in there and tell the gabachos (Anglos) to come over. 'Hey,' we'd tell them, 'we're going to invite you guys over to our foxhole for dinner.'

"This squad leader, he would call me Washington since I was from Washington and so was he. On patrol he would call me. He'd say, 'Washington, move up. Guard our flank. We're gonna go up and check this out.' He would sort of watch out for me and show me the ropes.

"He was from Kennewick and his name was Kenny Collins. He kind of watched over me. I saw him later at the community college I went to after 'Nam. I could tell he wanted to hug me. He had been in a wheel chair and had difficulty walking. He had only been in Vietnam three months when he got fucked up. I think he still thought of me as the new guy. I didn't want to tell him how I got the Bronze Star and the Purple Hearts and became platoon sergeant.

"He was walking but he had a lot of pain. He stepped on a mine in Vietnam. We were on patrol and this Vietnamese kid took off running and Collins got mad and went after him. He should have known better but you get mad, with that constant danger. You just get mad and want to get your hands on the enemy. There was this big explosion and we ran over to him. He was in pain. He just said, 'Washington, they fucked me up.'

"This was the same guy I saw barely walking at the community college. He still had a lot of pain, a lot of rage."

The Crater

"Once we were encircled all night long by the North Vietnamese. We had suffered some wounded and it was too late for us to get back to our position, so we took to this old bomb crater for protection. The NVA encircled us and played with our minds all night long. They would throw grenades in our direction to see if we'd react and give away our position. We remained where we were all night and what happened next occurred at dawn when the fog was beginning to lift.

"We could hear some feet padding around not too far away and we figured the enemy would eventually get close enough to get us with a grenade. Since I was the only one who wasn't wounded, the sergeant told me to go out there and get him.

"You've got to remember we were all huddled up together in this old bomb crater. Everybody was hurt and tired and getting a little desperate. We talked in whispers. I agreed to go, putting down my rifle and taking a grenade in hand. When I had climbed over the lip of the crater and past this log I suddenly heard something. I went out and swung my arm to throw the grenade, standing up in the process. The fog cleared in patches so you could see some trees and brush.

"Suddenly I saw the North Vietnamese standing to my left, not too far away and with his rifle at the ready. There I stood with my mouth open and my arm stretched out ready to throw the grenade at the noise in front of me and here was this NVA with an automatic rifle watching me do it. I watched his rifle barrel grow in size until it looked like a cannon. He had me cold; I knew I was dead and I couldn't swallow or move. By rights, I should have been dead, but instead he turned and ran. It was the spoon from my grenade that did it. I must have startled him. He must have heard the clicking sound and it saved me.

"Later they found a dead NVA with a hole in his chest, so I must have gotten one of them. The one I saw wore a gray uniform, leather boots, and a Marine style hat but more sloped. The one I saw had been even smaller than me but he had looked like a giant.

"I got on the horn and called in help and then I helped to carry some of the men out of the crater. Captain Wolfe put me up for a Bronze Star for helping to get the wounded men to safety."

The Lieutenant

"I was with Captain Wolfe for six months and had developed a good rapport with him. Then we got a Lieutenant Kinson [pseudonym] as the new CO (Commanding Officer). He was 20 21 years old, right out of Officers Candidate School, and without any real combat experience. He had been working with Captain Wolfe for maybe one month to learn the ropes, but hadn't come under fire during that time. He was short and blond, and he sweated a lot.

"One time while we were on patrol, Lieutenant Kinson told me to take a squad across this rice paddy. We had sensed something from the very start and I was reluctant to expose my men out in the open like that. He wanted us to cross in a line carrying the '60's with us. I told him we didn't do things like that in Vietnam, which of course he didn't like. After all, if you were a lieutenant would you want some E 5 telling you how to run your company?

"He really didn't like me to begin with so now he called me a yellow coward. He called another one of the men and said, 'Adkins, Alaniz is scared. He doesn't want to cross that paddy as he was ordered. I want you to take the squad across.'

"Well, by this time I had developed my reputation and the men knew me as I was under fire. They knew it was a lie that I was a coward. They also knew Lieutenant Kinson was wet behind the ears.

"Adkins looked at him and looked at me and said, 'If Alaniz is scared, then it must be the wrong thing to do. Don't look at me to do something Alaniz ain't willing to do, sir.'

"The lieutenant got really mad and flew into a rage. 'Isn't there a man in this squad who's willing to cross that fucking rice paddy?' he bellowed. He ran around asking each one of the men if they would do it and each one of them told him that if Alaniz wouldn't do it, they wouldn't do it either. Oh, man, I felt proud of my men when they did that. I'd been working with these guys for six months and we had gotten to know each other really well.

"What happened then is this: the lieutenant went up to several men to ask them to cross the field, but they wouldn't do it. About this time he came to Dewitt. Dewitt had been having his problems; his girl had sent him a Dear John letter. He'd been moping around dragging his ass. He wouldn't do anything and gave everybody shit. They in turn gave him a rash of shit and he had really been having a hard time. It seemed like everybody was down on Dewitt; in fact, it looked like the whole world was shitting on Dewitt. Well, then this ignorant inexperienced lieutenant ordered him to go across that field and Dewitt flipped him the bird and said, 'Up yours, sir.' Everybody laughed that somebody like Dewitt could make a fool of the lieutenant.

"Eventually, they did cross but not until they had set up the machineguns to fire cover for them. The squad that eventually crossed lost two men. We finally went around the field in two files."

Night

"Our Brigade had a system of rotation in which we took turns moving in column at night. We were trying to catch the enemy by surprise, but, actually, we lost more men at this time than we ever did during the day. It seemed like we lost a lot of men to accidents and to the bad terrain.

"One night I fell in this dike and tore my shirt. We had a firefight and were dug in. The moon was out, clear. I rubbed my stomach. I was hot and sweaty. I brought my hand up and saw the palm was bloody; it was shiny. I had ticks in my armpit and chest. I got rid of them but I couldn't piss, either. Found out I had a tick under my foreskin. It had gotten inside and got big drinking my blood and couldn't get out. I called the medic and he came and was embarrassed to touch me. I remember he had a flashlight and was poking around and trying to see what was wrong with me and the other guys began razzing him. Finally he stuck it with a pin and put insect repellent on it. But we couldn't live it down, cause the other guys went on saying stuff like, 'Ol Doc so and so was playing with Alaniz's ...'"

Day

"I still have a bump on my right brow that I got from a tick. Where did you find ticks? Well, we found them in the jungle where there was a lot of brush, a lot of leaves. You didn't find them in the woods where there were mostly trees. You found them in the rice paddies, but not in the elephant grass. The leaves of elephant grass were like blades and they were large and didn't contain any leaches or ticks.

"There were other pests in the jungle besides ticks. I got attacked by wasps once when I was cutting stalk, cutting a trail with my machete. Lots of times the Point Man cut a trail while the Second kept watch over him. These wasps stung me in the head which swelled so large I couldn't put on my glasses because they wouldn't fit. I looked like a Jap. I went to see the Doc and they gave me a shot that put me out for 24 hours.

"It might have been around this time that I got promoted and that my wife had our first baby. I got this picture of my wife and our baby girl and I couldn't bring myself to believe that it was ours. It was so strange and so far away. It was like I was looking at a dream.

"We had gotten married while I was in Basic Training. I asked the Army at Fort Lewis to let me go home to get married. I wanted to get out. Basic Training was a miserable thing. My family never had guns much and we never hunted much so there was just no way in hell I was going to ever be able to compete with these other guys who had learned all that stuff from their fathers. These guys knew how to take a gun apart and put it together again, how to pitch a tent, and all that stuff. If they didn't already know how to do it they knew how the system worked from having been Scouts and stuff like that. I had never been camping.

"Anyway, I got together a big stack of papers proving that I was the only support for the family because my dad had a heart condition. I appealed to them that my dad was in a bad way and that I was the oldest one in the family and would have to pick up the slack if he died, but they didn't listen. They wouldn't let me out.

"I got no break between Basic Training and AIT (Advanced Infantry Training). But during AIT, the Red Cross flew me home to get married. My wife was seven months pregnant. The Red Cross did come across for me. When we got married I was an E 1. My wife was 17 years old and I was 19. After that I went back to AIT and qualified expert with the M 60 caliber machinegun. The rest had definitely helped me get myself together.

"After that I didn't hate the Army so much. I started relaxing. My personal problems weren't so bad anymore. The only bad thing that happened during that time was that Richard Alsavido and I got caught sleeping under the barracks when we were supposed to be pulling weeds. The platoon sergeant wanted to give us an Article 15 (penalty less serious than a Court Martial), but instead I came out of AIT as an E2 rather than an E 3.

"After AIT we went home and then they sent us to Vietnam. I remember wanting to go with the same guys I had trained with. We went to Vietnam on the same plane but they then split us up. Everything happened so fast after that. My friend, Richard Alsavido got hurt somewhere in Vietnam; he lost both of his legs. I never did see him again. I kept writing to him until I got a letter back that said, 'No longer at the same address.'

"Richard's mom, Senora Alsavido, kept writing me and helped me out for quite a while. She sent me money and gifts. There was also this guy in the platoon who was rich and had gone to a military school. Once a week he would get these big packages which he did not want. He hated his parents and would give the packages to me or to other guys in the platoon. So I would get these big packages from this rich guy and crackers and tuna fish from Senora Alsavido. Dad would send me Devil's Meat and wieners.

"This rich guy never really got into any trouble that you could speak of but he never volunteered. That was one thing he never did. He thought the Army sucked and he never did more than he was required to do. He was an intelligent guy; he just had an attitude problem. You got the feeling finally that he had never had any love in his family. He talked about it, how his parents sent him away to school and never went to see him much. I got the feeling that he didn't have much love to give anybody, that he hadn't received much love and so he didn't have any to give anybody else."

Busted

"I went on R&R in Hawaii and when I came back I went out into the field again. I was shorter (less time left of duty in combat zone) than this other guy but he got an easier job than me. He got a job driving the colonel around. Another guy who had been in Vietnam less than me got a job as a bunker guard. They all started getting safer, easier jobs in the rear, all except for me and this black guy named Hamilton. I didn't feel it was prejudice but that is what happened. They told me there were a lot of Chicanos and Puerto Ricans in the company so I was needed there.

"Finally our first sergeant saw what was happening, how Hamilton and I were getting screwed, so he said he'd do something about it as soon as he got sent to the rear.

"Well, I was in the rear supposedly and I was sleeping in a bunker, and Lieutenant Kinson came by inspecting the guard. I had been asleep covered up with a poncho liner, and he thought I was a guard sleeping on duty. He didn't mean to kick me, he meant to nudge me with his boot to get me up. But I was asleep and didn't have my glasses on. I jumped up and hit him as hard as I possibly could and knocked him out.

"He came awake and yelled, 'Grab him!' and these two guys grabbed me.

"He asked me, 'What in the hell do you think you're doing hitting an officer?'

"I said, 'Why did you kick me? I was asleep and I didn't know who you were.'

"He answered, 'Well, I didn't realize you were so close to the wall. I didn't mean to kick you so hard.'

"He turned me in and he assigned an MP to guard me for the night while I slept. The next day I had to go see the colonel. That was on Hill 54.

"The colonel heard me out and understood what had happened. He wanted to help me out but he couldn't. The colonel said that I had acted wrong, that I had to show the lieutenant respect and start taking orders from this officer. I got demoted from platoon sergeant to squad leader. 'We can't let you off, Sergeant Alaniz,' he said. 'If we let you off hitting an officer, everybody in this damned Army will be doing what you did.'

"Because of what I did I had to go back out in the field as a squad leader. But the colonel had told me that I did have a job in the rear, that I was going to be a sergeant of the guard at the main entry at Hill 54 or Hill 69, our base camp. That had led me to believe my combat obligations were over. I had been out there eleven months and ten days. I thought I had done enough, but that wasn't the case. They had to make an example of me. It turned out to be the best thing that could have happened to me because the rear got hit and the bunker I was supposed to be guarding was wiped out.

"Because of the demotion and transfer to a different platoon, when I got back from R&R, it was like coming back to a different world. The first day they gave me new clothes. I looked like a new guy. 'Oh, no, not a new guy,' they said. They didn't want another guy to break in. They had thought they'd be getting an experienced guy.

"Then some guys in that platoon heard them. Guys that knew about me in the first platoon. 'Hey, this is the Chicano Audie Murphy, this guy'll do a job on you guys.'

"When the guys in the 3rd Platoon heard this they felt good. They heard how many awards I'd gotten, two Bronze Stars. Captain Wolfe had given me the Bronze Star for getting the guys to cover and pulling a guy out who was wounded. He also put me up for the review board for E 6 which I flunked. But I got Acting Jack Five. You know, a lot of things happened over there. Guys that were leaders got killed and other guys who should have taken over wouldn't do it. Even guys with college degrees wouldn't do it.

"The first or second day after we took off from Hill 54, one of the men in my squad who was also named Alaniz Benito Alaniz hit some kind of a tank mine. Benito had been in country only about thirty days. We had gone north from Hill 54, and then we cut south. We were walking on the road and we still near the villages. We had squads on both sides of the road.

"Benito was from Brownsville, Texas. Earlier I had promised him a wooden chest that I had. It was a real pretty wooden chest that I had and I had painted my last name on it with white shoe polish **ALANIZ**. It was worth about thirty dollars back then and back in the states it would have been worth about two hundred dollars.

"The only thing that was left of his body after he hit the booby trap was his chest cavity no arms, no legs, no nothing. And the helmet (we found no head, no nothing) was flat like a tortilla; the name tags, when we found them, all you could see was 'Alaniz' and a 'B' but the 'B' had been scratched out. Except for a few guys who were in his squad, everybody thought it was me that had been killed because everybody knew me to be 'Alaniz' since I had been there a long time, and as I said earlier, Benito had only been in country thirty days. When they called the name back to the rear, a lot of my buddies thought I was dead.

"After Benito was killed, we kept going on patrol and a day later something happened that showed me that even Lieutenant Kinson thought I was dead. He had called all the platoon sergeants and squad leaders up for a meeting before we were to go up to the main hill where we were ambushed. He saw me and he took a second look and he said, 'I thought you were dead!'

"I said, 'No, I'm still kicking, and hopefully, I'll make it.'

"He gave me a kind of dazed look like I came from the dead. I repeated, 'Not yet. Not quite yet, I got a few days left.'

"I spoke in a halting voice, kind of angry, because I knew that by all rights I shouldn't have even been out there at that time. But not that I minded because a lot of the men out there were my men and I still had respect for them and they had respect for me. They took the commands. Even though I wasn't the platoon sergeant any more, they would always kind of check back with me to see if the guy that took my place as the platoon sergeant was giving the right commands and making the right decisions. It probably wasn't fair to my replacement, but when you're in that position for as long as I was you gain a lot of respect from your men and they won't go back on you."

The Flak Jacket

"The day before we met where I surprised him by being alive, Lieutenant Kinson called all of the platoon sergeants and squad leaders together. He was giving an orientation for what we were to do the next day and what we were going to carry up the hill. Some of the men, I don't recall if they were my men or men from another platoon, had seen some kind of movement on top of the hill we were going to take, and we brought this to his attention. We did this because we wanted mortars fired in there or maybe a recon or gunships to go up there first.

"Lieutenant Kinson just said, 'Nah, don't worry about it.'

"So we went up to the hill and at the base of the hill we set up our perimeter for the night. We didn't get no action, no nothing.

"The next day we moved up toward the hill from our base camp. I forgot who was leading, but Gary Brown was the Point Man at that time. He was in a different platoon from mine at that time.

"Brown had the same time in country as I had. He had about twenty days left in his tour. Gary Brown was the type of individual who spoke his mind like I did. It was hard for him to take commands from guys who didn't know what the hell they were talking about. If it hadn't been for his big mouth, Brown wouldn't have been out in the field during his last thirty days . . . as I wouldn't have been either.

"He was out there because his superiors didn't like him because he always talked back. Even with that much time in the field, he was only an E3 or E4.

"Brown was from California, but I don't remember what town. He was a harelip, but he didn't talk like one. He had some kind of scar on his lip.

"There was an incident probably a month prior to his death. He wanted to pull point but he wanted to pull it without wearing a flak jacket. The Company Commander, Lieutenant Kinson, argued with him. Kinson told him, 'You're stopping the whole goddamned company from going on this patrol because you don't want to wear the goddamned flak jacket!'

"Brown hollered, 'It's too goddamned hot!' and it was hot. We had sweat rolling off of us. Brown said, 'I'm not going to wear the goddamned thing. If I get killed, I get killed, but I'll take my chances.'

"Lieutenant Kinson told him, 'You aren't going to pull that son of a bitch. You put on your flak jacket or you get the hell to the back!'

"Brown enjoyed pulling point, but one of the platoon leaders couldn't handle him so they had called up Lieutenant Kinson to intercede. I don't remember all of the details because I wasn't real close by when it happened.

"Lieutenant Kinson was still a 2nd Lieutenant when he took over from Captain Wolfe who had been our company commander for six months. Captain Wolfe trained Lieutenant Kinson by taking him on two patrols with him. But Kinson sure lacked the experience that Captain Wolfe had. I had all the respect for Captain Wolfe and I would have gone anywhere for him or done anything he would have told me to do. He's the one that gave me all my promotions that fast, too."

The Kill Zone

"Anyway, it was pretty obvious that there was some activity up on the hill. We'd seen it from the distance and reported it to headquarters. The orders came down to go up and check it out. Headquarters could've had the place softened up a bit with artillery, but they didn't do that. They sent us up instead.

"They sent two platoons up the hill. It was a winding trail with some elephant grass and scattered trees that got thicker in some areas. We were filing up on the trail . . . there were seven guys in my squad . . . six of them were killed instantly. The ambush was so fast that they just tumbled over dead in front of me and behind me. Guys farther up the trail were killed like that, too. The first blast also killed the Point Man, Brown, and his backup way up at the top.

"Then everybody hit the ground and started coming back toward us down the hill. Some men were being hit as they were running down the hill. Bullets were flying everywhere. I was about 200 meters from the bottom of the hill when this guy came running down, his eyes kind of wild. 'God, we're being hit!' he hollered.

"It was really chaotic. It seemed like the end of the world, but I got my wits together and got some guys to help me round up the wounded. There were lots of them. These were the ones left alive that couldn't run down the trail. There were a lot of dead, too. We found guys lying on the trail with no legs and one guy without a head. His brains were hanging out of his skull and looked like hamburger.

"I remember on the hill this Chicano from California got hit in the ambush. A piece the size of a saucer came off the back of his head. I found him on the trail and put the piece of skull back on and covered it with a scarf and tied it up tight and he took off.

"At one time I used to think I had been spared when others were killed because of my size and complexion, that maybe the enemy thought I was Vietnamese. I thought about it: why did I survive?

There were several incidents where I felt that way. Especially on the hill, though, because a lot of guys on my right side and left side were getting shot and killed and I wasn't. But now I see that a lot of other Hispanics were about the same size and the same color, and they were shot, too.

"The men in this new platoon where I had been transferred included one Cuban, a lot of Puerto Ricans and a few Anglos and there were a few Blacks, too. There were about fifteen Chicanos out of about twenty eight or thirty GIs in the platoon, so they made up the largest group. I had some Castillos, Baldemares, Balderes, Mencha, etc. So when we got ambushed, we must have lost quite a few Chicanos. But I don't remember their names or recall stuff like that. Over there the blood is all red. Color doesn't matter, whether you're black, brown, or white. Everybody's blood is the same color. When they bleed, they bleed.

"That thought that I was being spared because I looked different was just something that I had created in my mind as a kind of excuse. Why am I not getting shot and they are? When I did get my purple heart it wasn't because it was a big wound. It was only a little wound, actually. And it could have been from our own shrapnel or from one of their hand grenades I really don't know."

In a Cradle

"The enemy ambush party had been well set up. They really got us. Some of our people were coming down on their own and others were being escorted down the hill. About that time one of the platoon sergeants, the one that took my place in my old platoon, came down the trail holding his chest. He was the type that wore his rank and a camouflaged scarf. He was walking real slow and he said he was hurt bad.

"His name was Carrigan (pseudonym) and I didn't like him because he really rubbed it in when he got my platoon. I wanted my platoon back. They had just left him there, and I went up and talked to him. I made him sit down and put a plastic patch on his chest wound. He had been shot by an AK 47.

"I tried to get him up from where he was leaning against a tree. He was a big man. I was going to throw him over my shoulder in a fireman's carry but it wasn't proper because he'd been hit in the chest. Instead I carried him in a cradle like a baby in my arms, and I don't know how many steps I took about three, four, or five and he got shot right in the middle of the head. His mouth opened up and he got another slug right there. Blood poured out of his mouth and got all over me and he grabbed me by the shoulder and neck, and he squeezed hard and bridged like a wrestler he arched all the way up and he pleaded, 'Don't let, please, please, don't let me die.'

"For a split second when he got shot I thought, 'You asked for it' then I caught myself. But there is no denying I felt that way for just a second. Then I caught myself. I think more than anything he didn't want to be left alone. I didn't know what to do. I still carried him down a few steps and I was going to take him all the way down, but then there was a lot of yelling and screaming from other guys. So I laid him down and went down the trail escorting other wounded men. I took a few men down to make sure they made it all the way down. When I got there, I talked to Lieutenant Kinson. I said, 'I want to go back to make sure about the guys on top of the hill. I want to see whether they're dead or still alive.'

"Nobody volunteered so I took these three guys with me but they ran back. About that time something in me snapped, and I remember going through a sort of mental motion in which I took out the picture of my wife and baby and said good bye to them. I knew I was going up to the hill to do my job or die trying to do it."

From Within Me

"I kept moving up the trail past three or four dead guys on the way. These guys were close to the top. One of the dead was Brown, the Point Man. He was about twenty meters in front of me, face down. I could see his boots and his back, lying in the grass. I just had time to glance at his body and at the others who had been shot on the trail in an open spot.

"I was walking fast at a crouch. I stopped in the high grass near to the open spot to listen. If I fired my weapon they would know where I was. But I didn't really get to make a choice; a burst from a machinegun ripped away my ammo clips and webbing. The springs and metal just sort of popped out. The bullets tore holes in my shirt between my arm and chest. Then I got out the two grenades. I ran some more at a crouch. I knew they couldn't see me. They knew I was down there beneath the bunkers, but they couldn't see me and I wasn't firing my weapon like a new guy might have done. They threw a potato masher at me, a bamboo grenade with a handle on it. It came sailing lazily towards me but it didn't go off. Then I threw mine, first one and then the other and ran back down the hill.

"The whole time I was up there I felt detached from myself, like I was watching a movie of myself. Actually, it was more like a stark black and white documentary of myself. I felt dazed; I had removed all the feeling from within me. It had become a game, like it was animals that were being shot. It was as if my old man was shooting one of the pigs or a cow all over again like when I was a kid. That was the only thing my mind would accept to explain what was happening out there. I made my mind do that.

"It was like when I was a wrestler in high school and had to run a lot of miles every day. I controlled my pain by thinking about other things like fruit, grapes, girls, anything. In 'Nam I had to use my mind to survive. God, I'm glad I was able to do that. Other guys had to take drugs, or drink. I didn't have to do it then. I was the only Point Man that didn't have to do it.

"It was during this ambush that I caught a piece of shrapnel in the leg and didn't know about it till the next morning. I caught this little piece of metal that caused a lot of pus. When we called in artillery on our position there was a lot of shrapnel flying around. One piece came by and cut this small tree in half. If I hadn't bent down to reach for something, I would have bought it.

"Later on I told my dad and he said he had seen me during a time of prayer. He had been praying in church and had seen me out there and he told the people in his church to pray for me. Apparently, God told dad that I would make it, that I wouldn't get killed, and who am I to say he didn't?

"When I got to the bottom of the hill after that close call at the top, I guess I was a little bit crazy. The guys said I was crazy. I was yelling at them, called them 'chickenshits'. I was raging mad and told the lieutenant that, 'these fuckers ran out on me.' The fuckers were the three guys that started up the trail with me but turned back. 'We don't want to end up dead like those other fuckers,' they hollered. They weren't giving an inch, they wanted to live, and they didn't mind telling me so. I guess it was like suicide going up there.

"The lieutenant told me to shut up. He said, 'Cool down, Alaniz.' He didn't exactly slap me around. I don't recall what it was he said, or whether they had to hold me back from those three guys. The guys I trained in my old platoon wouldn't have run, that's a fact. A lot of them were dead. Maybe that's why I ran back up there."

A Second Ship

"We called a chopper and those who could walk got on the ship. I was on the hillside watching all of this. There were about 14 wounded, including the FO (Forward Observer, a lieutenant) that had to be ferried out by chopper. This officer really impressed me because he refused to get on the chopper before his men. They were all fighting to get on because there were so many dead and there was the feeling that we were surrounded. The FO still refused to be carried on board before his men.

"When the ship started to rise, the slugs from the enemy positions started slamming into it. We were right there and could hear them piercing the metal, hitting it with a violent impact until the helicopter exploded into a fireball right in front of us. All those wounded who fought to get on were wiped out, blown to pieces. They had been fighting and yelling to get on board. That's what saved the FO's life, that he gave up his place for his men. I think that's what saved his life. Later, a second ship came down and they put him on that one and he got out alive.

"Before the second chopper came down, the FO called in artillery right down on top of us. He had to do this to save us from being overrun by the enemy. Earlier we had rounded up a lot of the wounded and put them in an old bomb crater. We did the best we could for them, but the artillery got them. Afterwards when we went to see them, they were all dead. They were just guts and brain all over the crater."

The Sky

"I'm a squad leader and I'm cutting some small trees so we can have a clear field of fire. We're sitting on top of this mountain. It's drizzling and we're all wet, tired, and sad. It hasn't been too long since the ambush and we're all a little disillusioned by it all. I'm pragmatic like I always have been and with my machete I'm cutting away some tender trees and some branches and grass. I'm busy at work and can see the men on the peak, sad silhouettes, lonely and cold. There isn't much talking; they're all depressed. The fog makes it difficult to see the enemy below. Yet, we're supposed to see them, that's why the men are huddled around the machinegun emplacement on the peak.

"Suddenly I'm thrown through the air. Rather, I'm surprised, manhandled by some absolutely overwhelming force, some giant hand of sheer power. I've been struggling to put my machete back in its scabbard, and out of frustration I've struck this rock. Suddenly I'm lifted and tossed in the mud. Wandering around disoriented, I find my glasses (they are all muddy) and look up in time to see the men going through a frenzied dance of pain, wildly arching and grabbing their backs and legs in agony and running in circles. It is a soundless world, the shock of the lightning bolt has deafened me, but my ears pop and suddenly I can hear their hollering.

"I guess that's what did it. We called in a Medevac to take out the wounded and the dead. Joe Reynolds who had made it through that ambush on the hill died here from that lightning. That's when I began to have my troubles. After that I became confused and started drinking. Before that happened, I used to believe that anything that came from the sky was God. But this was such a negative force and it played against such odds that it made me wonder what my own odds were for making it out alive from Vietnam. I began to figure that if God wanted you dead you were going to die no matter what. You would die from this lightning, ambushes, or snakes. You would die somehow. I began to pray and to ask God to save me. I promised to go to church."

Stateside

"Later, after 'Nam, this captain kept giving me shit details. This was in the barracks stateside. I complained to the general and made an appointment to go see him. I told it to him straight, 'I was trained to fight. I'm a hero and should be treated like one and not the way I'm being treated.' The general called in the captain and told him, 'This is one of the best men we've got. I don't want to hear you treating him this way.' He chewed his ass out royally.

"I just couldn't play the game stateside with all their rules and bullshit. At the time I had never been in front of people except during the real thing. I didn't know how to stand in front of people and teach. They tried to give me a chance, but I had no background. They told me I'd be busted from E 6 to E 4 unless I got up there and taught. I said, 'Fine.' I couldn't get in front of people."

An Afterthought, 1985

"What I said earlier concerning Lieutenant Kinson was true. But after being an officer for a while now, I can see that he was under a lot of pressure. If he was not my age, twenty one or twenty two, he was probably younger. I, myself, was a platoon sergeant and I was about six months to a year older than a lot of the men I did command. A lot of the time I acted as a platoon leader because a lot of the platoon leaders had died while I was there. About three or four were killed during my tour in Vietnam.

"This is really hard for me. What I stated earlier is still true from an NCO (non commissioned officer) point of view. Now that I'm an officer and have been an officer for two years, I've had different roles and different responsibilities. Even though my experience as an officer has not been in a combat role, I have had a lot of responsibility in training men down at Fort Benning. So when I think back, I imagine that it must have been a big responsibility for a twenty one, twenty two year old like Lieutenant Kinson to command a company, to be totally responsible for all of the individuals there.

"Like I said, in Vietnam I was responsible as a platoon sergeant for twenty eight or thirty guys, and when you have those conditions we had over there and have four times as many men to lead, like Lieutenant Kinson had, you could get a little edgy.

"I never realized it back then.

"But I still think I could have done a better job myself. But you know, it was a different time. It's water under the bridge now."

Chapter Two

On the Blind Side

Carlos Ramirez
1969 - 70
4TH Infantry Division

"We kept track and found out they were assigning us the most dangerous positions on the blind side of the camp. If we got hit, we would absorb the initial attack and suffer the casualties." Carlos Ramirez

Survivor from Armored Unit
The Smell of the Dead
First Casualty
Old Sergeants
The Bird Sang "Fuck You"
The Latin Squad
Breaking Squelch
Ben
The Intensity
Maggots, an Afterthought

Survivor from Armored Unit

"This guy was stuck with an armored unit. You had to talk loud to him 'cause he couldn't hear you. He had been the only survivor in this unit that had been wiped out. The guards fell asleep. This guy was heavy into drugs, spaced out. He told stories to make your hair stand on end. It was hard to believe he was for real. He drifted away during conversations."

The Smell of the Dead

"The first day in the field we received fire. We were flown from Pleiku to the area 1/2 hour by chopper. Roughly three to four new guys were split up with the veterans. I had a strange, funny feeling; I was scared but not before the firefight. It was there afterwards.

"It was dense jungle that we cut through with a machete. They put me in the middle of the squad and we walked about two klics (kilometers). We had a blue line (stream, river) to cross so a guy with a rope had to swim across. A guy on a shrub stood security for the guy swimming. We had one guy on each side of him with an M-60.

"The third guy to swim across received fire and that caused everybody to fire back for a 'mad two or three minutes'.

"We killed two or three of their guys. Sergeant Kelly could tell what us new guys were feeling. He took us over to one guy who had part of his skull knocked off. He said, 'This is it.' The '16 bullet did that 'cause it tumbled when it hit you.

"Those dead must have been there quite a while before they got killed. They were not strac (Military acronym: Skilled Tough Ready Around the Clock). They wore ragged clothes and smelled bad. The smell, I always remember the smell. I found a blanket much later and it smelled the same way. I could always pick up the smell afterward. Sometimes a week would go by with no action, then I'd pick up the smell."

First Casualty

"It happened when this guy went out to defecate. We were humping the boonies with these guys called Roger's Rangers. They were careless and not worth a shit. Our guy made it clear that he was going out to defecate, but when he got out there and was coming back into the perimeter, these guys saw the bushes move and killed him. He had been there about five or six months so he wasn't green. It didn't happen because he was careless.

"Another time we received fire and called in 'Red Leg' (artillery) by phone. We either got a short round or had called in the wrong coordinates, because our own shell killed two guys from Seattle."

Old Sergeants

"When I was at Ahn Khe, we didn't have to worry very much because it was a cleared area. We didn't have to patrol a lot. But at the Firebases, you had to set up at night to catch the enemy in case they tried to assault. You carried your maps with you so you could plot the coordinates and preset your artillery support.

"If the enemy came in really close, we called in gunships to rake them over. But if they were a little farther out, like 300 yards, we would call in artillery. You started the shells falling out a ways from you and then called them in closer. You tried to use a large landmark and to draw two points that way.

"A lot of the time we had an artillery officer with us who would preset the coordinates and call in artillery. But I didn't trust them. I trust the E-6 who had been in the army a lot longer.

"When we were out in the bush, I liked to set up near a tree in a wooded area where we could see the trail. The best place was where the trail angled because you could have a longer view at somebody coming up at you. These things were all taken into consideration and also the kind of cover available when we set up. At times we would use a 60 caliber to cover or we would use claymores or both.

"Our company didn't carry empty sandbags for fortifying our position when we set up, but we did have to take a turn at the pick and shovel. We dug in.

"The company operated as a unit, but sometimes it would split up and the platoons would stay at least 1000 meters apart. That was so they could get artillery support without calling it down on each other.

"You know, the whole time I was out there I never ran into any old sergeants, but other guys always talked about them. These old guys knew a lot of ways to get you out of trouble, but I never saw any.

"Most of the time that we saw action, it was 'cause we ran into the VC or they ran into us by accident. Lots of times there was no evidence of any contact. Three times we captured only one person. One of them was wounded, about seventeen years old and really scared like I would have been if they had captured me.

"I spent a lot of my time out there dreaming about home and what I was missing. I told myself I wasn't going to mess around when I got home. But, no, I don't feel that I went through any big change when I was in Vietnam."

The Bird Sang "Fuck You"

"Before I went to Vietnam, I thought it was an ugly place. A lot of poverty. But after I got there and things began to fall into place, I could see it was beautiful even with the poverty. I hadn't expected mountains, just rice paddies. I was amazed at the heat when we got off the plane.

"One of the first lessons we got was to avoid an open area if at all possible. When we had to cross such an area, we spaced ourselves out. For part of the year it rained an awful lot. Then when the B-52 (Air Force bombers) made their Arc Light strikes, the sky would light up like lightning and you couldn't tell if it was thunder or not.

"We were out there in the boonies and we would find this bird that made a quick sound like 'fuck you'. It seemed very appropriate when you had that disgusting rain and cold all of the time.

"You know, you learn a lot of things over there, and a lot of it stays with you. When I'm hunting, I never sling my rifle. They ask me why I don't do that, but I never explain it to my relatives. If it's unslung you can turn quick and fire. I got a buck that way. You find yourself using the same tactics you use in Vietnam like you ... don't make any noise, you don't trip over limbs and you don't misfire.

Sgt. Carlos Ramirez, 4th Infantry, Ahn Khe, Central Highlands, Vietnam.

The Latino Squad

"When I was with the unit out of Ahn Khe, I was put in charge of a Latino squad. There were Puerto Ricans, Hondurans, Mexicans, and some Negroes. The Puerto Ricans were 'crazy'. They gave me the impression they didn't care. I'm not making a general statement -- this is just about the guys in my squad. Of course, in a firefight it was different. They really put out and held up their end.

"I got to know this Puerto Rican really well who was from the States but had spent a lot of time in Puerto Rico. He talked a lot about Ponce, which I think is in the middle of Puerto Rico.

"Then I had this guy in my squad who was from Honduras. He would always kid me about how he was going to take me home to marry his sister.

"Puerto Rican tamales are good, you know. They wrap them up in banana leaves, not like us. As you know, we use corn husks. This guy from Ponce used to get a lot of stuff from home. For Christmas he got these tamales that were made of rice and had garbanzos in them. Then he got these plastic jugs full of rum with coconut milk. It was good.

"Then there was Jose Fonseca (pseudonym) who was short, about 5 feet 3 inches tall, and was always talking about the ladies.

He was always combing his hair like the Fonz. These guys all had more time to go when I got wounded; when I left, that was it . . .

"When we were moving, like when we went in to Cambodia, it was a good feeling to have two maps. The jungle got pretty thick. Some places you could cut through with a machete, others you had to extend these long pipes with explosives; we called them bangalores. We'd use them to blow a path in a really thick area. But they wouldn't hurt the really big trees. So if we wanted to knock down a big tree, for whatever reason, maybe to open a field of fire (so the enemy would have a harder time sneaking up on us), we would use some C-4. That was the same material we used in claymore mines. We would use it to dynamite the trees.

"We also used it for cooking when we ran out of heat tabs. The heat tabs give you a lot of heat with a tiny flame. You couldn't build a big fire because the enemy snipers would see where you were and pick you off.

"Our time in Cambodia was a hot, muggy, miserable one. We were in the mountains with a lot of trees, a mangrove forest with lots of vines and brush. It seems like it was 10 to 15 degrees hotter than it was around Saigon, or in Pleiku where we had been.

"One thing we noticed that got our ire up was that the command was screwing us. We kept track and found out they were assigning us the most dangerous positions on the blind side of the camp. If we got hit, we would absorb the initial attack and suffer the casualties. The guys noticed it and began to complain. Why weren't the other squads getting that assignment? Why weren't they rotating the most dangerous assignments? I took it up with the platoon sergeants and they said ok, and they began to rotate the duties.

"We were at this little base camp called Camp Anarry. We were taking these stand-up baths outside, all naked, going crazy with the soap, you know how it is after you've been in the bush for a long time. It was during the monsoon, I remember that cause you got used to listening for thunder but this time somebody yelled, 'Hit the dirt!'

"We heard that at the same time that the AK-47 rounds went off around us. Then it stopped as sudden as it started. We got our rifles, but there was no more action. As usual, the guards had been shootin' the bull, not paying attention, listening to the radio.

"I suppose a well-placed round could have gotten us. The bunkers were cleared of any trees, any obstacles for 300 yards, so I suspect they could see us as well as we could see them. But we were out in the open.

"One time it was late at night and we received fire. We had come in from patrol really late, too late to do any digging. It was hard, rocky ground that resisted the work of your entrenching tool. Mortar rounds started coming in and everybody hit the ground. We had been exhausted but now we hugged the rocks tight. Then Jose Fonseca panicked. I guess from the rounds coming in so close. Three of them came in really close, you could see them flash 'cause it had been pitch black and late at night. Fonseca started yelling, 'We're going to get killed!'

"I grabbed him and the guy from Honduras helped me and we tried to soothe him and calm him down. I was scared too, but we knew a thing like that can get out of hand so we held him down. After a while he was all right."

Latino infantry soldier waiting for resupply. Central Highlands, Vietnam.

Breaking Squelch

"In Vietnam, they would send us out a few hundred yards beyond the perimeter to catch any of the enemy trying to approach the base. The damn fools inside the perimeter, our own guys, would send up flares with their mortars. We were out there in the dark and we heard this canister go off and there was a flare! We hit the ground 'cause everybody, us and the enemy, could see everything for 150 to 200 yards out. We were sitting ducks.

"Sometimes we would get a request to go out 500 yards, but we wouldn't go. You took a chance going out that far cause if something happened ... There were nights when I or nobody wanted to go out there. We'd let them see us going out, then we'd sneak back in. We would 'break squelch' (call on the radio) every half hour to let them know we were out there, that everything was all right.

"The platoon sergeant himself used to sneak back in, so why shouldn't we? But this guy blew it for us. The way we did it is we would get to our location then call in. But this guy was spaced out and called in, 'We are now leaving the perimeter.'

"A second later he called in, 'We are now set up.' That sucker blew our cover and we had to spend a night out in the bush when we could have spent the night in the bunker.

"But that was the big problem, the reason we were reluctant to go out at night, 'cause of these guys that would be spaced out.

"The guys had times when they would be pissed off. I remember we walked 11 klics (kilometers) once and had to use mine detectors to clear the road for the APC's (Armored Personnel Carriers) and so it kind of tired us out. We finally got to this village and they brought out this 'Panther Piss' which was what we called rice wine, and we spent the night in the village partying. You had to do that occasionally for the guys.

"Lots of times we would hump the boonies then have to dig bunkers after we were already exhausted. It's hard to explain. We would secure the site, you know, establish fields of fire, call in coordinates and all of that. Then we'd kick back and call in some marking rounds for the artillery. Sometimes the guys would be tired and wouldn't want to dig the bunkers and so I would start doing it since I was the squad leader. I dug my share of foxholes and bunkers and I also walked point a lot when I didn't have to. It was dangerous to be the first one on the line, but you couldn't get the men's trust if you weren't willing to do those things yourself.

"Other times we would make assaults on ground that had been shelled by artillery. The broken tree stumps would be pointing up like barbed stakes and the door gunners on the helicopters would be pushing you off -- and here you are weighted down by a hundred pounds of gear. You would go down like a lead balloon. Well, I learned fast to throw my pack separately and hold on to my rifle. If I made it I figured I could always make my way to the pack.

"Those helicopters, they were our link to the outside when we were in the bush. Later in the States when we'd be hunting in the mountains and we would hear the thud, thud of the helicopter blades, I would say to my cousin, 'Hey, Sal, here comes our resupply.' We would share a closeness in our response to that, you know the laughter."

Ben

"We had a Kit Carson Scout, a Vietnamese who had been with the North Vietnamese or VC and had come over to our side. I don't remember what his name was but everybody called him Ben. I remember the guy always wanted new boots. He had a fascination with the Black Market and was always trying to get us to buy him new boots.

"Ben was always fresh as lettuce when we were marching while the GIs would be all worn out and sweating. The guy was 44 years old. At the PX (Post Exchange) back in Pleiku, we would get whatever we needed. But of course, Ben would be there wanting those new boots. I kind of felt sorry for him because he really didn't ask for much, considering that he could keep us out of trouble in the bush, but the GIs didn't trust him, didn't like him and would call him 'gook' and 'VC' and generally shove him around.

"One of our sister units stumbled onto an entire company and were wiped out. They were just a platoon. Then later we uncovered a large bunker complex. They had this little prison there, a bamboo stockade for the prisoners with a place for your head and arms and legs.

"I guess all this sort of thing made the American GIs nervous or angry, because sometimes they would mistreat their Kit Carson Scouts. You know, they would push them around and call them names. They didn't feel comfortable putting their lives in their hands."

The Intensity

"When I got back to the States I was a loner for a while. Other guys found it easier to fit back in when they got back. I guess that's the way it goes, you know; the minute I got to Vietnam I knew what was going on. You learned a lot about life over there because you didn't have everything you wanted or needed. I'm rambling now, but that's the only way I can talk about it 'cause it all ran together. We were living a different life in 'Nam. I miss the people I shared my experiences with. There is no one around and sometimes it gets to you. Sometimes people who didn't know what was going on over there, they wanted to talk about it and when you tried to explain it to them they didn't understand it. It was usually useless to try to explain it. Do you know what I mean? It was difficult to explain.

"When I got back, I didn't want the same intensity I experienced in Vietnam. When I went to parties, you know -- before Vietnam I had this attitude where I didn't care, I didn't give a damn about things. When I came back I did care, I just wanted to be mellow. I didn't want too much interaction; I just wanted to be mellow, to avoid hassles.

"If the ladies wanted to go out with me as if I was a hero, that was to my advantage. I didn't have the problem other veterans had when I got home. I had been wounded and people treated me real well and wanted to talk about Vietnam. Maybe it was because I live in Idaho or maybe it's because I'm Hispanic. I don't know. But I didn't feel any of the hostility other vets talk about. When I went in to see what kind of services were available for veterans, the VA reps really wanted to get into talking about Vietnam, what it was like and all that."

Maggots, an Afterthought

"When I came in to Cam Rahn Bay, I got assigned to a shit-burning detail. We had to pull these half-barrels out and pour diesel fuel over them and watch them burn. It was enough to gag a maggot and I guess that's why the drill sergeants call you 'maggot' during Basic Training, because they want to get you used to living like one. That shit-burning detail was a pretty good introduction to the Vietnam experience.

"Then I spent two weeks hanging around the beer parlors at Cam Rahn Bay until I got assigned to my field unit.

"At Cam Rahn, I got the basic issue like helmet, fatigues, rucksack, first aid pack, poncho liner, poncho, air mattress and entrenching tool. Later at my field unit, I got the grenades, claymores (mines), flares, trip flares, canteens, and C-rations for four days. I got my M-16 rifle and 400 rounds of ammo which I learned to wear Pancho Villa style draped on belts across my chest. This was typical GI style.

"So we ended up carrying from 80 to 85 pounds and sometimes carried an extra mortar round or maybe 100 rounds of M-60 ammunition for the machine-gunners. An M-60 was a big gun that normally required that you carry 2,000 rounds for it, so we would split up the hauling of all this ammo. Then we also tried to fight the heat by carrying 6 quarts of water apiece and fought twice as hard not to drink it all.

"I almost forgot about the night scope. One sniper moved with each platoon. This guy used an M-14 rifle because of its larger barrel and its steadiness. Otherwise our equipment and weapons were pretty standard except for the Point Man who carried a 30 round clip with his M-16 or five shells for his automatic shotgun. If something happened, these guys had to put out some fire quick and had to have these weapons available."

Chapter Three

Imagine a Mountain

Carlos Ramirez
(Second Interview)

1969-70
4th Infantry Division

"We had set up an ambush and it more or less backfired on us."
Carlos Ramirez

Send Up to 'Nam?
Three Busted Toes
A Chicano Drill Sergeant
There's a Road
Carmel and Seaside
Cam Ranh Bay
West of Ahn Khe
Thirty-six Choppers
Try to Visualize a Mountain
A Maturity Thing
A Real Nice Ride
Talking About the Anniversary
Outside the Third Herd

Send Us to 'Nam?

"I was drafted. I had no choice. I thought of going to Canada! (A chuckle)

"It's really strange. When Joe McGuinn (pseudonym) and I went to Washington to catch the bird to 'Nam, we were actually thinking of going AWOL (Absent Without Leave). You have so many days before you have to go over, so we decided to go into Seattle and have a good time. We went into town and they had to come and get us and put us on the plane.

"The MPs caught us uptown. They had pictures of what we looked like 'cause we were still in military garb. They just approached us and said, 'Hey, we've been looking for you guys. Let's go.'

"We figured, 'Hey, what are they going to do to us, send us to 'Nam?' (Laughter)

"We were only gone for two days. They know when someone is missing because every day they have a detail, whether it's picking up cigarette butts or whatever. But for being gone for two days, they didn't do anything to us. A little lecture, that's about all."

Three Busted Toes

"That day when I broke those three toes during Basic Training I knew something was wrong because it started hurtin' a little bit and all of a sudden it all went. The drill sergeants didn't believe me that there was something wrong with my foot. So they tried to make me run and I couldn't. They did it because they had so many guys drop out of formation, but I never did drop out of formation when we were running. That day they ran us with a full pack in the sand.

"I couldn't go anywhere so finally they came up there and they got me going. I still ran about a half a mile back to the barracks. There at our barracks they had an oval track which is a one mile distance. Once you got back to the barracks, you took off your pack and ran another mile before you went in. So I ran that mile too, and when I got inside the barracks, I just blacked out.

"Before I knew it they couldn't even take my boot off so they just sent me to sick leave with three busted toes. (Pause) I think I could have sued 'em." (A chuckle)

A Chicano Drill Sergeant

"We had Advanced Infantry Training (AIT) right there at Fort Ord, just over the hill. We lucked out in the drill sergeant we got. It's strange how I kept lucking out during this whole experience. It was like a string. I kept hittin' the right places as far as the training. Our drill sergeant was a Chicano from Houston, Texas and we got along real good. As a matter of fact the day before our AIT was over he bought us all a case of whiskey. He was real mellow, once you got to know him. You know a lot of the guys didn't like him, but once you got to know him, he was alright. He was of medium height, but to look at him he didn't look like a drill sergeant at all. He looked too mellow.

"Maybe it's because after seeing the ones in Basic, these were Teddy Bears. But this guy, he was pretty good. I think he knew we were probably all gonna go to 'Nam and he got to know us on a personal basis. There were just certain guys that he would talk to on a personal basis; the rest of the guys he would holler at. But we used to get away with a lot of bullshit. I think it was mainly because we got to know him."

There's a Road

"There were night courses we had to go through with a compass. There was no way you could cheat because we tried it. They give you a course that you have to navigate with your compass where you have to go to certain points and you have to write down what was at these points. That's the only way they knew that you'd actually done it.

"We had another night course where they would simulate Viet Cong and take you to a place where they could torture you. If they caught you they were supposed to torture you. It was a course you had to pass. There's a road that makes a loop around the area, and we just stuck to the road. A bunch of us got together because if you got caught you had to spend the whole night there. By the time we got back to the barracks it was already about midnight. Then you've got to get up early. So we figured, 'Well, let's make the course ... quick. We'll go over to the road and then we'll just go over to the truck and tell 'em we made it.' We just waited to make it look like we went through. We didn't want to get there too soon.

"Other guys would come wandering in around two, two-thirty in the morning and had to get up at four-thirty. It was just a means of survival, I guess, to cut corners.

"AIT was no where near as bad as Basic. We didn't actually specialize with any particular weapon. They showed us how to use the M-16, the M-14, the M-79 grenade launcher, the LAW, the M-60 and we even used the .50 caliber. The LAW is an anti-tank weapon. The M-79 is the one you put a little canister in.

"When I first got up there to 'Nam I didn't know how to used trip flares because that's when I broke my toes in Basic and that's when they covered that. In 'Nam, they had to show me how to use them. I remember thinking, 'What the hell is this?'

"But the one thing in AIT that they emphasized was how to read your compass because that's the only way we got from one point to another up there. Otherwise, we didn't know where we were half the time."

Carmel and Seaside

"Whenever we could, we'd go to Carmel and Seaside. It was just a good release, besides the fact that the Carmel and Seaside area is just really a nice place. It's totally different from anything around here. It was just a release to get away from the whole military thing.

"We were noticeable as GIs because of our hair and manner, but I didn't get any negative vibes from the civilians. I noticed that more when I came back from 'Nam and I was stationed at Fort Lewis, Washington. We'd go to Seattle and you'd always see somebody trying to get you to blow some money on a lady that they'd be pimping. They'd try to take advantage of you. It didn't happen so much at Carmel, though, because the people were so used to seeing so many Army guys around.

"One of the nice things about AIT was that we knew each other. In Basic Training you're still trying to figure out all of these different faces from different places and you don't really know whether to trust them or not. Once you got into AIT you've spent all this time with them and gotten to know them to where it's a lot smoother. When we'd go into Carmel it would be a mixture of browns, blacks, and whites.

"After AIT I got 30 days leave at home and then went to 'Nam."

Cam Ranh Bay

"I'll never forget the first time we hit Cam Ranh Bay. When we first went in, that's the first place we landed. I remember stepping out of the plane ... it was as if ... like somebody hit ya cause of the heat. I thought the heat was just too much. It affected me, but one thing I did do ... I ate a lot of salt. I had to, to keep my strength; it gave me strength. The heat, jeez, it was just unbearable.

"As far as keeping it together, the only thing I found that kept me together during my tour was that *I really wanted to come back.* As a matter of fact, we'd be out just about every day, traveling really slow 'cause of the vegetation and when we'd stop my mind always had a tendency to wander and I'd be back here in the States. I think that's what kept me going, because I just wanted to come back and I'd get to daydreaming about a coke and a cheeseburger, fries.

"You looked for ways to keep it together. Like wearing the metal helmet that was protection from shrapnel, from stuff flying around. For that reason the weight of the helmet didn't bother me. The mosquitoes and leeches didn't bother me much because I found out that it was the guys who were too lazy to carry a lot of bug juice that were bothered by them. Those guys wouldn't go through the hassle of really tying down their pants over their boot so that the leeches couldn't get in there.

"They would know we were going to go into places where there weren't very many blue lines (streams) to get water and yet they were always going short on water. I probably carried a heavy pack, but I carried a lot of water and a lot of bug juice.

"As far as drugs, I got loaded three times, but this was when they brought us in from the field. I think a lot of guys got loaded to escape from reality. The reason I didn't do it is that I didn't want to get away from the reality. I think thinking about the reality is what kept me sharp. I didn't want to take any chances, that's how bad I wanted to come back, if that makes any sense."

West of Ahn Khe

"We were west of Ahn Khe on a mission, and there were a lot of villagers that came in and wanted c-rations. They were really hungry, so we gave rations whenever we could.

"There was this girl that would always come around and tell us whenever there were VC in the area. We would be on patrol along the perimeter and this girl and these people would be there to the side.

"It was one of those occasions where we had built up a relationship, and where there seemed to be some trust. I think I could trust her whenever she would let me know about activity in the area.

"After they disbanded the 135th, I didn't see her anymore, because we moved on closer to Ahn Khe. With the 135th we used to work closer to Pleiku.

"With this girl, it wasn't like with the others because with the others you knew that that (c-rations) was what they wanted. This little girl had more than the rest. The others were really down (trodden) whereas this girl was at least wearing clean clothes. There weren't very many little kids like her that owned a bicycle.

"There are times when something about Vietnam is shown on tv, and I get to thinking back and that's one of the things that I remember. It seemed like it was a good relationship. I think a lot of people, when they think back, think about the bad things. That's probably natural for some people but I think back about that little girl. I wonder if she ever made it or whatever happened to her."

Thirty-six Choppers

"I'm not really sure what happened to the second little girl I wanted to tell you about. The 114th, the unit I went to later on, was involved in a big insertion into Cambodia. There were twenty-six or thirty-six choppers lined up to transport troops. These kids got caught up in the movement of troops because they were trying to get c-rations from us.

"I don't think that what happened to this little girl was intentional. She got caught in the middle of that. A lot of people didn't seem to care whether it was an adult or just a kid that was totally innocent. Some guys had it in for them simply because they were Vietnamese.

"It was just an incident that happened where a guy started kicking a little kid. It may have been that he kicked her more than once. There were a lot of things happening all at once. When you're in a place like that getting ready to board the choppers, there's stuff flying around and it's noisy. I could be mistaken, but I think the GI kicked her more than once.

"That's when I hit him with the rifle butt. It's like I've told you, there were jerks. I hit him and his helmet went flying and he fell. In this instance nothing was said because I was a sergeant. Not that it meant a lot but he was a private, so I had a little pull. It was an incident, an aberration, that shouldn't have happened.

"Maybe the guy wasn't that bad of a person. I really didn't get to know him well. You never got to know anybody real well. You know, when I first got in-country, the guy that gave me my orientation told me, 'Don't get to know anybody real well. That's in case something happens.'

"You never really know anybody. Whenever you were out in the boonies, you never really did talk a lot because you were supposed to be real quiet. You kind of knew the guy next to you just as a person right there, but that was all. I went from one unit to another, but I never got to know the guys well except for four or five people.

"A death over there is totally different from a death over here. There it happens and you do what you have to do. You call in to have the body taken out and you go on because you have a mission. Sure, you feel bad, but you get over it real quick because you say to yourself, 'That could be me.'

"In the back of your mind, you're always telling yourself, 'I want to go home.'

"The guys that did get killed, I didn't know them real well. I knew they were there. I think a lot of the guys were like that; it wasn't only me.

"To see somebody dead in Vietnam is a totally different experience to seeing somebody die here. Over there you are living with death all the time; you're only waiting for your number to come up.

"Now that I've been home a while, some things will happen to trigger my memory and sometimes it seems like those things I remember never happened. Maybe it has to do with the passage of time. Sometimes it seems like those things never happened, but they *did*. Maybe it's that a person is trying to forget."

Try to Visualize a Mountain

"I had been in 'Nam ten months, two days when I got wounded. We had set up an ambush and it more or less backfired on us. (A mild chuckle) It backfired because we knew the enemy was in there, and we more or less knew where the route was, and we hit that right on the nose--how they'd be coming down; but by the same token we didn't know that there were more of the enemy above us on higher ground with mortar rounds. They started mortar rounds on us after we opened up on the guys on the trail. The ambush seemed like it lasted a long time, but I would imagine that it only lasted ten minutes. It lasted long enough to get the artillery to hit them back ... but it's hard to say because everything happened so quick.

"Try to visualize a mountain like this (he lifts one arm), and coming down like this and then we were like this (Carlos lifts the other arm parallel to the first) on another little ridge and then from that big mountain there was a little trail trickling down like this. For some reason we knew that's how they would come down. The enemy with the mortars were above us, the VC on the trail were walking toward us, and we were off to the side but all three elements seemed to be in a straight line. As soon as the Viet Cong on the trail came down, we opened up on them. The VC were pretty much out in the open, but they had to go around this great big rock. When they went around that rock, we lost a few of them. We couldn't see 'em anymore, we just couldn't see 'em, they got around that rock. But the majority of them we could see when we hit 'em.

"To tell you the truth, I couldn't tell you how many we got because everybody was scrambling. But there had to have been anywhere from seven to a dozen, I can't remember it now. It all happened real quick. Everybody was trying to shoot, and it was really weird.

"The first couple of minutes everybody figured we got it made, we'd done our job. Then all of a sudden, you can ... if you've ever heard a mortar, you know what's happening (Carlos makes a sound like 'toup' which is like the surprise uncorking of a wine bottle followed by a tiny, spiraling whistle). The mortar rounds started dropping around us and everybody hit cover.

"I can visualize the minute I got hit because I was sitting on an incline, and -- for a split second -- I saw my leg sticking out from behind this tree. It was like something said, 'That's a no-no.' All of a sudden I saw that chunk of metal hit me, and it just knocked me back. My rifle flew out, I looked down and my leg was *all bloody.* I was in *pain!!!* I tore the pant leg off. Somebody yelled, 'Get a medic!' I looked down and the calf muscles were dangling really weird. They gave me a shot of morphine and after that it fixed me right up.

"I was the only GI that got hit. There were about sixteen of us at the ambush site. Our platoons varied from fifteen to twenty-five men, depending on how many were coming in to replace the ones that were leaving.

"Most of the mortar rounds were actually hitting below us. It was the shrapnel that hit me, that shot up and got me in the leg. Nobody got hit, but while I was in the hospital still in 'Nam before they shipped me to Japan, they said that the VC dropped (destroyed) a chopper going out the next day. It did kill some of the guys that were in there.

"I don't think that the guys received more support. More than likely they were instructed to stay there and check out the area. We had different units on different ridges to catch the VC, so ours wasn't the only unit there. It did kill some of the guys that were in there.

"I knew the enemy were VC because they had on what looked like cut-offs. Raggedy cut-offs, and they all had on a baggy shirt and they didn't wear a hat like the NVA (North

Vietnamese Army regulars). The NVA that I saw wore a uniform, and these guys didn't. I remember that there were two of them carrying a basket full of rice for their meals. They were definitely VC."

A Maturity Thing

"The change that I went through in Vietnam was more of a maturity thing, and I'm not sure if it was so much rage or anger. But there was a change. The one thing that used to get to me--and I think it made it harder for all of us--was that we didn't have the air support that the other units had.

"We of the 4th Infantry Division were probably one of the worst units when it came to getting air support. A lot of the other units had all the choppers they needed, and if they needed support from planes, they got it. If we needed a plane to come and bail us out, they had to come from Chu Lai, and you know that's quite a ways. These other units, they'd actually fly them out hot meals! We never did get this kind of support, it was a rarity. Yeah, we got 'em once in a great while, but it was a real rarity.

"I can almost visualize it now when we went into Cambodia. The 101st Airborne came in and looked at us and thought we were crazy because of all the stuff we were carrying. All they carried were their weapons and ammo. They told us that every night the helicopters would bring them out whatever they needed wherever they set up.

"I remember we came into this field. Most landing zones were covered with tree stumps because they had been cleared by explosives or chainsaws for landing choppers. I remember they came in to drop us off, and that when the chopper gets near to the ground you bail out and drop to the ground. At the same time, the 101st was bailing out and I just happened to notice this guy, and that's when he said he couldn't believe all the stuff we were carrying! It was just a real quick conversation and then you're gone, everybody goes one way or the other. Once you bail out of the chopper you go to your assigned area and they go to theirs. I never did see him anymore."

Sgt. Carlos Ramirez (on right) and fellow Hispanic GI with the 4th Division in the Central Highlands, Vietnam.

A Real Nice Ride

"When I got wounded they put me on a stretcher once the little Loach (a type of small quick helicopter) came in. They had a little Loach come in because it was real dense (woody) and they couldn't get a regular slick in. They came in on a Loach and I remember them bringing the stretcher. But once the medic gave me that shot--he was on me so quick to give me that shot, he really did a good job--that once that thing took effect there was no pain and I was **LOADED!!** In my mind I was so loaded, but I could hear the guys say, 'Ah, you got a million dollar wound, you're going home.' I just remember the voices telling me, 'Ah, you've got a million dollar wound, you're going to be all right!'

"They took me back to Ahn Khe. I even remember the ride back on the Loach because I was so loaded. Yeah, I was so loaded, and I remember the ride because it was like a real nice ride and everything was so mellow.

"They patched me back together at Ahn Khe. I was there just a few days, but I was stoned all the time because of all the medication. From there I went up to Camp Drake in Japan and spent anywhere from twenty days to a month there. That was what was weird, that place. By then the wound was getting better and I was on medication, but not as much. I could see what was happening, guys yelling at night, and even during the day, from pain. It kind of reminded me of a graveyard. You know the guys were bad (hurt).

"I don't remember how long it was, but they let me call home from the hospital in Japan. I told 'em I was alright, I was in the hospital, and I'd be coming home. I tried to minimize the impact because I didn't want them worried. I just told 'em I'd gotten hit in the leg and I was alright, I'd be coming home. I didn't want anybody to get all excited. I remember Gonzi telling me that my dad was really upset. That was quite a hospital, Camp Drake.

"I went to Madigan (hospital) in Seattle and I still wasn't able to walk. I still had to go to physical therapy because when I went to Japan they operated on me again. Now (June 1985) I only run two miles a day, maybe five days a week. I do it mainly for my leg because it feels better when I keep it active rather than just laying around putting on weight. I wish that I could run ten miles, but you know, I'll run two miles and my leg feels pretty good. If I go three, I'm really pushing, and my leg starts to bother me. Two miles is just right for me. I hate to run, but that's the only thing that keeps me in shape. I lost my taste for running in Basic."

Talking About the Anniversary

"There were a lot of Latinos in Vietnam. That's the one thing that really got to me when they began talking about the anniversary of the Vietnam pullout. Every time I saw something in the news, everybody they interviewed was always white. And it really bugged me because they made it seem like the only ones that were up there were white people. Shoot, you know when I was at the 1st with the 135th and I went with the 1st Corps Team, I usually got all of the Latinos. I had whites and blacks too, but I got the Latinos because we could communicate better and things went a lot smoother. And there was a shit load of 'em up there! Then I see all this on the news; they talk about the people that were over there in 'Nam and how they're having problems. They only show white faces and it kind of makes me angry.

"Even here locally, they interviewed several different people because this thing (anniversary) went on for some time.

"I tried going to the DAV (Disabled American Veterans). But I found the DAV to be--I don't know if it's like that everywhere--mainly the older guys that are involved. I've gone to a few of their meetings and it's kind of like a turnoff in a way because there aren't that many people that you can actually talk to. You know they're doing a good job, and they tried real hard to make you feel welcome but it was just different.

"The guy that signed me up wanted me to see if I could get some other guys to sign up. I talked to a few of the guys; they said they'd think about it but they never did, so why push it if they don't want to? I think the only reason I joined is 'cause this guy that got me to join was a pretty nice little guy. He made a lot of sense and it kind of inspired me to join."

Outside the 3rd Herd

"I haven't seen Joe McGuinn since the last time I attended BSU (Boise State University). He was going to BSU to be a nurse. That was in '73 or '74.

"We went through Basic and AIT together, and through the same division, the 4th Division, but we were in different companies. He came home about a month after I did. You see, I was about to complete my tour when I got wounded; maybe I had about two months left. No, no, wait a minute, I take that back. He (chuckle) ended up in the same unit that I did in Fort Lewis after I had to go back and serve the rest of my time. He ended up in the 3rd Herd, too. That was so weird. As a matter of fact, I've got pictures of us that we took outside the 3rd Herd area. That's strange ...

"I never thought they'd take that guy. He had a record like you wouldn't believe. He asked for extra paper to put all the shit he'd been caught with and put in jail for."

Chapter Four

He Started Thinking About Vietnam

Sergio Armijo

1966
U.S. Special Forces

"You survive, along with other white guys, you survive. And they scream, and they yell, and they cry, not that I don't cry and scream. But they do the same thing that you're doing." Sergio Armijo

South El Paso
Nothing Happened
Airborne
Not Our War
Yeah, I'll Eat With You

South El Paso

"I think at one point I'm saying, 'Ok, so I'm first generation immigrant. My mom comes from Mexico. All her family had been back there, except for herself. She comes across.'

"When I joined the Army and I'm dealing with the white system, obviously--I shouldn't say obviously, but you can assume that most of them are second, third generation Anglo Americans in this country -- versus myself and maybe the other guys, Chicanos, Mexicans, that were with me ... It's been how many years now? '66--twenty years ago. That's a *long* time. Twenty years ago I was in Basic Training at Fort Bliss. And I get my *first real exposure* to white people. By that I mean ... in high school I really didn't have to deal with them because we were all Mexicans.

"I think one time I went to summer school because I flunked algebra. The teacher said something like, 'You'll always be a Mexican.' It pissed me off. I don't know why he pissed me off except I didn't like the way he said it. I closed the book, I flunked. So the summer school I go to was El Paso Technical. And they're all white. And I don't fit, which is no problem 'cause all you do is go to study one hour, an hour-and-a-half, summer school, get out, and go home.

"But I knew for the first time I was in an environment of all whites: it was *very, very* different. I may have been a sophomore then. I had to travel across town from South El Paso to the middle of El Paso. All of the kids there were white except for two of us who were Mexicans. We had khakis and starched shirts and all these guys looked different: Levis, tenny runners, cowboy boots.

"I knew there was a difference; and the difference is more pointed when you go into the military because there *you have to live with them.* Then you start gettin' all this...

"I went into the military about a year, a year-and-a-half after high school. What happened is that I had been working in the grape fields in California during school. So I graduate, I say, 'What the heck, I don't know what I'm doing.' I tried for college. They said 'No.' I didn't do good on the test, so I went back to California. By now I wasn't grape pickin', I was loading trucks. But then I got a job offer from El Paso in a print shop.

"So I go back. They were all Chicanos in the print shop, except for the managers, and staff like that; they're white people. And that doesn't last long because again, I've been trained to be a printer and they put me to sweep floors. I couldn't handle it, I just couldn't handle it.

"In high school you would go a half a day to print shop school and half a day to regular school. As far as I was concerned I was a printer so I wasn't going to sweep floors for no one. I quit that job. It lasted around a week, and then I took a job with the El Paso National Bank. And there I'm doing a little bit of printing, but at least it's more a print type of work. I'm enjoying it more.

"But then, late December or early January, you read the newspaper where it says you have to enlist or we'll draft you. You're eighteen years old, that's it. There's no lottery then. You just have to register, they needed so many bodies. 'We're going to get them one way or the other.' You were getting drafted--period. You were not married, you were not in college, you were getting drafted!

"This was '65, '66. So I decided rather than have them draft me, tell me what to do, *I'm* going to tell them what I want to do. So I enlist and I hitch up for three years. I wanted to be a clerk, which never worked out. I didn't have the background to be a clerk.

"Going back to Basic Training, you live with these folks and they're asking you all these questions, 'What if we go to war with Mexico, are you going to join them or join us?' This was at Fort Bliss. In my platoon, they were about ninety-five percent white and maybe four percent Mexicans, and maybe one Black.

"For the first time you realize you're different. I didn't realize I was different. Back in high school, going to summer school you realize that you're different because you dress differently and you don't fit with them. You've never lived with them. You've always been a first generation immigrant living next door to Mexico. But now they're asking you questions--the kids, their kids, right? They're asking me dumb questions: 'What if we go to war with Mexico? Which ...?'

"Now you start realizing you're different. You can't really conceptualize it. Let's say, 'Well, I'm first generation, I speak Spanish, I'm Catholic, therefore I'm different.' Questions like that

... or just racist terms used against Mexicans or Blacks. Or the fact that certain things don't make sense. The aggressive nature against other people because of their race or 'We're going to go kill gooks, or we're going to go kill Asians' or whatever the words they were using. There was no longer a fight, just fighting, it was more like fighting a *different race*. And I was starting to figure out that I was a different race; if not a different race, at least a different nationality.

"And that caused a lot of problems in terms of trying to fit in. I didn't really fit in. Till *today*--I don't fit in. I think I can say that. I know I'm different.

Nothing Happened

"After Basic I went to AIT (Advanced Individual Training) at Ford Ord. It was Clerk AIT. The transition was the same. Again, they put you in the barracks with all these white guys. I was still a naive eighteen-year old.

"The idea is to isolate yourself. That was *my protection*. I didn't talk to them. I'm still at that point where I'm trying to figure out 'Who am I? What am I doing here?' As a clerk, as a person, as a soldier.

"In AIT, I had clerical school. So it was more civilians, women, teaching you to type, do filing systems ... teachers ... No, they didn't single me out for harassment. All things considering, it was easy. In terms of actually dealing with pin-pointed racism, you didn't have it. But I had learned enough to stay away from it or to just not deal with it. My drinking was by myself.

"That's one of the interesting things. In Basic Training I hung around with one guy who couldn't speak English--Daniel. He had it rough. I don't know how he dealt with it. He was out of it. He didn't know what the hell was going on.

"He got harassed a lot because he didn't do it right. Like they'd tell him to do one thing and he didn't know what they had asked. He got more KP, more being yelled at because he would screw up. And he didn't even know what the hell was going on. Pretty soon they came around, 'You speak English, you speak Spanish. You stand next to this guy. Any time we say something, translate.'

"So here we are at AIT, and I'm doing clerical school and he's doing advanced infantry. And I've been there maybe a month or two, and sure enough I meet up with the guy. So we start going out drinking. So I can associate with that guy ... I think he worried a lot. He started thinking about Vietnam before I did. He knew if he went out there, he could get his ass shot ... till today I don't know if ... He was infantry. 'What's going to happen to me? It looks like Vietnam; they're saying so many guys are going to Vietnam. Would I be one? Sounds like it. Could be. I don't know.'

"I'm able to hang around with this guy. Have a few beers whenever we can. But I couldn't deal with the white people. I remember them coming into the barracks and being loud. They'd been out drinking. It pissed me off ... because they were loud. To me drinking beer is one thing. The other thing is to be just damned loud. These guys would just come in making a big deal out of it. I remember taking on two guys, saying, 'Fuck you.' Just for the heck of it. They probably didn't address their jokes at me. But just the fact that they were loud. 'Fuck you.' Pretty soon I had two white guys in front of me. We were going to get into it.

"Nothing happened. But I didn't feel comfortable. And I think that goes on, further on. I don't know what's going on, I don't know what I'm going to do, whether I'm going to be a clerk or what. There's airborne school...

"I don't know if I was conceptualizing, if I was up in my mind enough to realize what was happening. The *people bothered me more than the system.* I knew I was a soldier and I knew I probably would end up being a clerk and maybe even go to Vietnam. That was part of the system. It was just having to deal with these people on a daily basis and having to talk to them.

Airborne

"There were some sergeants, lieutenants, coming around to talk about airborne. I signed up. I got signed up for it. Then from then on I knew I was going, and I started running every day. That's when I realized that I'm not the . . . that running wasn't my bag because I couldn't stay up with the rest of the guys. I smoked, I drank, and I couldn't stay up with the rest of the guys. Towards the end ... maybe. After a month running I could probably keep up with them. So I ended up at airborne school at Fort Bragg. And it's the same thing.

"I wasn't a part of anybody's group. It was just me. I knew I could do it. The hardship was exciting. I like the excitement. The idea of jumping out of an airplane. I didn't know what it would be. But it was fun.

"I heard of guys being kicked in the shins because they wouldn't jump off the towers, but I never saw any. If you were that nervous, you were pulled back. The major problem was making sure the harness didn't catch your balls when you slipped on the thing that pulls you back. You made sure the thing was wide open. Otherwise, you had problems down there. But that was exciting to know that you were going to graduate and be a paratrooper. That was exciting.

"I liked airborne school. I like the running. I liked the discipline. You're up at four o'clock in the morning, so at five, six o'clock you were in bed because you knew you have to get up real quick in the morning. You're always running. You're always ... you have to react to situations . . .

"I ended up in Da Nang. I don't know where I came in. I think it was Bien Hoa. I don't know. That was a big place. I ended up with 5th Special Forces in Da Nang.

"I think in my situation, I think that Vietnam was a positive point in my life. I think I learned ... one--physically--*el gringo* is no better than we are. At some point in our lives, I think a lot of us doubt that. They're a little bit taller ... Whatever it is, we get paranoid ... But you go through Basic Training; Basic Training--I could have done better--I didn't know *how*. But the idea of kicking ass, I could kick ass with the pugil sticks, right? I was pretty good; they chose me to represent the platoon because I kicked some ass. Then I lost, my problem. I just didn't ... (he points to his head) up here. It had to be up here. I wasn't doing it right.

"Vietnam, you see all these guys get shot at, and they're dying. Who's doing it? They're these little fuckers, this big (indicates how the Vietnamese are small-framed). They're doing it. They're shooting your ass off. You survive, along with other white guys, you survive. And they scream, and they yell, and they cry, not that I don't cry and scream. But they do the same thing that you're doing.

"That helped me to understand a little bit about myself. You go to airborne school, that helps you too. The end result is that you come back here and you say, 'Can I do anything? Can I go to school? Yes, I can go to school. Can I do this?' Realizing that you're different. You're somewhat singled out. Vietnam was a good experience. It definitely was. If I would have stayed in El Paso, without going to Vietnam, like a lot of my friends. You know, one way or the other, I got out of it. They're still doing the same thing. Is it good to stay in the same environment and do the same thing? It pushed me out of it. It pushed me out of where I had grown up, where it was nice and comfortable and I didn't have to deal with problems, *other* type of problems.

"I think in Vietnam I could *definitely* start seeing a difference, how they treated Vietnamese. I say *they* 'cause I never ... never had the balls to treat Vietnamese the way a lot of white people treated Vietnamese. Racism ... the words they used to describe them. The way they would treat them as people, socially. Socially, they were less than you were. They could not come into your taverns, they could not do this, they could not do that.

"I think what I experienced as a kid growing up in this country was made very vivid. It was there. Because these people were definitely different. Slant eyes, short, different color.

"The anger, the resentment, the idea that I'm different ...

Not Our War

"When I was getting ready to go to Vietnam, the attitude of my friends was, 'Are you going to get your ass shot off? What's going to happen to you?' But more interesting to me, was my mom's perspective of things. An immigrant--very little education—but she brings out ... she says to me, 'Why are you going to fight other people? Did *you* start the fight with them? Did *we* start the fight with them? No, it's the government. The government should be fighting the wars, not us, we're just people. You and I should pick up our belongings and go to Mexico. That's where we belong. It's not our war.' Maybe she didn't ... in her own way she was making a damned good point.

"The idea was what the hell was I going over there for? What was I representing? The American way? *What* American way? South El Paso way? That was different! Hey, live and let live. We're different, you're poor, I'm poor, we're all poor, so big deal! We just live.

"Whereas these guys had this concept about capitalism; it works! Capitalism changes your lives into this and that and that. That's not true to the majority of the people over there. In Vietnam, or to us in El Paso. Things don't change. Why? Because of our background, because of who we are. Because the ... guy doesn't let us ... Many different things like that. We are what we are.

"Here in Tacoma the class is the Blacks. We have Blacks all over the place. And *they are* the bad people. They get involved in crimes, they don't work, they're on welfare, they're *bad*. So it's the same thing as pinpointing people in El Paso or even in Yakima. The poor people are the bad guys, not educated, not ...

"You know it's a strange feeling. I go back to Yakima. And once I'm in Yakima, I'm like this (lifts forearms and elbows to ward off imaginary blows). I'm waiting for some idiot to say something stupid. In Tacoma you can blend in a little bit more. Sort of, sort of, but it's there.

"In Tacoma, I play around with it (ethnic jokes), maybe too much. I go off and get drunk with Tim and some other guys. There's one or two guys that are always yakking their mouths off. 'Green card here.' You play around with it but there's only so much. There's some of it you resent. It's there.

"I was going back there (Vietnam) with my buddy from back home, Tony Diaz. You might want to talk to him. He's got the same deal, he can't speak (English). Well, sort of. Anyway, I met him. When I came back and I was going back for another hitch for six months, my friend was also going back there for his first hitch. Tony Diaz was going over there.

"I came over here after a year in Vietnam, then I wanted to go back ... another six months. I wanted to go, I volunteered. We were in El Paso together. I'm trying to remember whether he went back after his first hitch ... I don't think so ... he was in straight combat the whole year. So I don't think he would have gone back. But somehow we spent a whole month in Mexico. I came from Vietnam, I had a month to kill. I went to Mexico and this guy went with me.

"We knew we were coming back together, somehow we were going back together, and somehow we just picked up our bags and we went to Mexico for a month. Then we went to Vietnam.

"We didn't carry our leave papers with us. But I remember buying a ticket for the train, gettin' on the train, and we were gettin' in Chihuahua, Zacatecas and the conductor comes up and says, 'Where are you guys (going)?' Here's these guys with no hair.

"We said, 'Ah, we're just going to go visit.'

"He says, '*Son Mexicanos*?'

"'*No, no somos.*' We're not Mexicans; not from this country, we're not.

"He says, 'Do you have papers to be here?'

"'Papers?' Dumbshits.

"'It's going to cost you five dollars to fill out these papers to show that you are visitors in our country.'

"'Oh, ok.' So we fill out some papers. For the first time ... again, reinforcement ... hey, you are different. You're not Mexican, you're not American. They give us little papers to carry in our pocket. We go to Mexico, we come back. A beautiful month!

"We were in Zacatecas ... Veracruz. I had $700 and the other guy had $500. We blew it all. We were drunk. We were drunk half of the time. No picking up ladies. We didn't hit. You know, you look like a GI. We went to cathouses, just get laid. Quite often. We were dressed in civilian clothes. I've got some pictures of that.

"We had a big argument. We were eating dinner one night with Tony's father in Mexico. His (Tony's) half-sister was there, and she brought her boyfriend. Tony was from Texas but his father was from Mexico. And Tony's half-sister brings her boyfriend over, and he's a college kid. He starts saying all this bullshit against war, against the Yanks, and ... hey, you've just been a year in Vietnam, you're not goin' to roll over just because some asshole is telling you how evil you are. So I had a big argument with the son-of-a-gun. For the first time--that I can recall--I defended the war in Vietnam. 'We're helping them, we're helping them, we're doing this, and we're doing this,' and this ol' asshole got on my ass.

"I defended it on a gut level because I had been over there dodging bullets and this asshole, this college ... little pimp ... was not going to tell me what was right and wrong.

"When I got to Vietnam, the idea was capitalism versus communism. We represented a system that was good. Whatever that meant ... it was good. They were poor, obviously they had a problem. We were going to help them. That was probably as far as I went. Communism, as far as we were concerned, was evil. Communism was enslavement, communism was non-democratic, and we went after their ass for that reason.

Yeah, I'll Eat With You

"While in Vietnam, again I separate myself. I had girlfriends ... Vietnamese. I eat their food, I speak their language, I get off base as many times as I can, I go with them. Now a lot of these people are Chinese. They are more educated and more into ... they can deal with you better.

"'Hey, you're Spanish from Spain! Hey!' They would snap their fingers and make like a Flamenco dancer. They'd clap their hands. They'd see that was a little bit different, but I can get along with them. Same thing with the Vietnamese ... I can *sort* of get along with them.

"I felt comfortable. You know how an American will sit down and eat foreign food and go, 'Ooh! Ooh!' I would sit down and eat that rice like it was unbelievable. I would eat their food, I felt comfortable. It didn't bother me if there was flies, maybe it's 'cause we have flies back home.

"The guys were nice enough ... I remember this guy took me home, introduced me to his maid, a Cambodian, 'This is so and so. You sleep here. She sleeps with you tonight.'

"I got along with them fine. I used to like it. I used to like the idea of just dealing with them. Talking to them. They'd bullshit a lot because they would expect you to know their little games and things.

"We were not allowed to go into the city of Da Nang. We were restricted, but I used to go there one way or the other. There were several ways to get out. You'd hide inside the maid's truck. At night they'd clear the Vietnamese out of the base, so you'd get inside the truck, either on the floor or hang to whatever--just get out.

"At the gate, the Vietnamese guards would check the vehicles but they didn't give a shit. Then we had to go through an American Marine base. The MPs were Marines, dumb-fuck Marines. Our camp was here and their camp was here, and we had to go through their camp to go to downtown. Once we got out of our gate, any hassles we'd have would be with the Marines.

"Fucking Marines. Dumb fucks. They actually grunt. That's why we called 'em 'jarheads.' They'd actually grunt and bang their heads against the wall when they'd be drinking. Six of those fuckers caught me downtown (I wasn't supposed to be there) and beat the shit out of me. Marine MPs, they put the cuffs on me and took turns hitting me. I'll never forget. The one that hit me the hardest was a Black guy. He must have thought I was white. I don't know. I don't know. But no marks, they didn't hit me in the face. All in the stomach and ribs.

"Anyway, this guy that invited me to his home was an interpreter, Mr. Ming. He was an interpreter; he was sort of like a bartender inside our company, inside our little base. I got along with him damn good. He was going to get married. They were sort of having a good time. He said, 'Why don't you come over to my house?'

"I said, 'Sure, I'll come over to your house.' So before we hit his house, he takes me to a couple of restaurants, a couple of stores; he says, 'This is my store.' His wife-to-be is selling clothes there.

"I say, 'Nah, let's go over here. Let's eat.' So we have some egg rolls and stuff. *Real good food.* And all the people there don't know who you are. They think you're strange because you're an American sittin' there. I had on civilian clothes and I'm also almost six feet. Most of those guys are 5'7", 5'5". But I sat there and ate these french rolls, I'll never forget ...

"About one-third of the people could speak French. They all say, 'Parlez-vous Francais?' I'd say, 'Nah, nah, I don't speak that shit.' But they'd want to start off that way, especially if you looked a little darker. I had a good time.

"I think they knew who I was. The name was different, and also the fact that a lot of times when they tried to be funny or play around, they would indicate they were playing *las maracas*. They'd clap their hands. So I was different. I think the important thing is that it never went up to my head that I was an American. They were Vietnamese, I was American, therefore I'm better than you are. That never happened to me.

"I remember taking a Vietnamese to dinner with me to our messhall. She worked there. She was one of the secretaries. I asked her to come over and eat with me. To me it was just a friendly gesture, and nothing funny about it. 'Let's go.'

"'Yeah, I'll eat with you.'

"And we walk into the messhall and the sergeant, the guy in charge of the messhall, came up to me. 'I can't serve you.'

"'You can't serve us? Why not, I'm hungry. I wanna eat.'

"'She's Vietnamese.'

"'What do you mean, 'She's Vietnamese'?'

"Again, I realize I'm different and I forget that she's different. I had been there maybe a year. I say to the guy in there, 'I'm going to pay for it. Why can't you serve her?'

"'Because she's Vietnamese.'

"'What's 'Vietnamese'?'

"'Well, because we don't allow Viet ...' He actually said, 'We don't allow Vietnamese.'

"By this time she's embarrassed, looking down into the table. Embarrassing as hell to her. But by this time, to me it's *an issue*, and I make a big deal out of it.

"There was no yelling match. 'I don't understand this. You serve her. She's another person just like I am. You . . . you're goin' to feed us -- right now.'

"He says, 'We can't do that.'

"I say, 'You better.' I was an E-4 (laughter). An E-4 telling a sergeant he better do that! -- he did.

"He served her, he served me. He just said, 'Ahhh! All right.' He rambled, and somebody else came out with a plate of food for her. After a little bit of confusion they served her. The people that served in the messhall were all Vietnamese.

"Another time, it was interesting ... again, this black-white thing. I'm gettin' drunk there with a Black, I don't know his name. A big, big guy. I thought he had insulted me when he said, 'You guys don't understand me.'

"'What do you mean?'

"'Ah, you . . .' I don't know if he said 'white.' He said '*You* people don't understand me.'

"I don't know what this fucker's talkin' about. I said, 'I don't know what you're talkin' about' -- and I said it in such a way that all the white guys tried to be nice to this Black guy. And we get into this big argument 'cause I kept askin' him, 'What the fuck are you talkin' about? We're gettin' drunk here and ... I don't understand your implication that we're all discriminating against you.'

"That comes on further on down the line where I used to have a good relationship with the Blacks, 'Hi' . . . 'Hi' -- that was good enough for me. And 'Hi' to the whites. Blacks would stick to their little ground, the whites would stick to their little ground and I would walk right down the middle.

"I didn't like the Blacks because I thought ... to me . . . they were making a big deal out of somethin' that I didn't understand. And the whites had their own little clique, and I just stayed away from everybody else. Again, one time I'm gettin' drunk with one Black, and big . . . again, maybe loudness bothers me, people that are loud. This sergeant comes out yelling, 'Ahhrr ahhrr, VC' -- or some shit. I said, 'Why don't you shut your mouth up?'

"And this Black guy's there with me. Anyway, the white sergeant says 'Well, I'm gonna take you on right now.' He comes at me--I'm 190 pounds now and I think I was 200 pounds then. He tries to bear hug me to the ground and he can't do it. He picks me up, or *tries* to pick me up like this and he can't and I roll 'im over. And I land on top of him. I'm holdin' him down this way and he's not punchin'. Neither am I, I'm half drunk, I'm just holdin' him down.

"He's sayin', 'I'm gonna kill you, I'm gonna kill ya' -- but he's not killin' anybody. I'm on top of him and he's not doin' anything. And the Black guy -- after the whole deal (they came and separated us), the Black guy says, 'You did the right thing. You did the right thing.'

"It came to a point where a sergeant tried to screw me over. I was not a real clerk because I couldn't type very good, I didn't know how to file very good, and I didn't really know the procedure very good. And one sergeant says, 'Will you take over my QC? You take care of my deal (duty) tonight and I'll take care of yours on Tuesday' -- or something like that.

"'Fine.' So I did it, then it came his turn, he didn't show up. So next morning, five o'clock in the morning, Sergeant Major brings us both in.

"'Yeah, it was my turn but he said he was goin' to do mine because I did his.'

"'Nah, I never said that, Sergeant Major.'

"This fucker's startin' to screw me over. So I said, 'Well, bring the other guys that were there. They know I pulled QC the other day and it was his day and he was supposed to do mine.'

"So the Sergeant Major brings other people, other witnesses. They come up and say, 'Yeah, Armijo's right.'

"And he (Sergeant Major) says, 'I want you out of here. Where do you want to go?'

"'What do you mean?'

"He says, 'Which of the A-teams do you want to go to?' That's combat (Sergio chuckles). 'Which of the A-teams are you going to?'

"Even though it was not my fault, there was enough little waves in there that they wanted me out. I said, 'Well, I want to go Mobile Strike Force.' That was it, *the place* to be. If you wanted to see action, it's Mobile Strike Force."

Chapter Five

The Vietnamese Knew
Something's Happening

Sergio Armijo
1966
U.S. Special Forces

"They didn't rush me. There was some dead bodies, they were picking up the weapons from the dead. They walked up maybe three feet away from me . . ." Sergio Armijo

The Walk in a Morgue
The Lead Truck
The Chaos of War
The Joking Stopped
We're Winning the War?
The Waste of War
The Vietnamese Ate Rice, I Ate Rice

The Walk in a Morgue

"I was still with the A-Team at Da Nang. The work was somewhat clerical.

"A couple or three weeks before that some people were hit, some people were dead. They wanted me to go pick up bodies at Khe Sahn. They sent me out there and the Marines are all in foxholes. And the chopper lands and right away they push us into foxholes.

"We run to a morgue to look for this one Vietnamese guy that I'm supposed to pick out to bring back and bury him. And I walk into the morgue and they're all Americans. That's sad. That *is* sad to walk into a morgue and see all these big bodies there. There must've been around forty of them.

"It's cold in there. They have the generators going. It's a cold room. You walk in and they have all these bodies there. You walk up to the sergeant or whatever he is, 'I'm looking for ... whoever.'

"He says, 'We have no Vietnamese here.'

"'OK.' So I walk back out again. All the time I'm looking at all these dead bodies. It was very disturbing. You could tell they were Americans, but you couldn't tell what race or anything because they've got them in bags. But they're big bodies. That's sad. I walked out of there and they took us out on some choppers. We didn't go back to the camp. We went back to Da Nang.

"You start fearing. You start fresh ... afraid. And that day we were there we were gettin' hit.

The Lead Truck

"Sometime after that I started gettin' into combat. I think the first time they sent us in with a convoy to another camp. We went in and came out.

"They told us where we might get hit. We went through it, dropped off the supplies and were coming back. We go through a hot section, through the hot area, and nothing happens. On the way back I'm stepping on the gas because I'm the lead truck. If we get hit, who gets hit first? The lead truck, to stop the rest of the convoy. I'm stepping on the gas and I'm going through this winding road, I remember it, I remember it. I'm going and I see this shell there in the middle and I maneuver around it and I'm pointing and the Australians, they're back there laughing. They maneuvered through it. We get back. Some time after that those two same Australians got into a firefight. They both got killed. Dead.

"Both of those Australians were Special Forces . . . in their own way. They were mocking me, they thought it was funny. They knew I was new. They just thought I was a little bit too shaky. For one thing, in their truck they had people in them and they had some stuff with them. In my truck I was the only one. So if the thing goes, you go by yourself.

"Why did I get the lead truck? That's a good question. The Australian captain in charge told me to be first. There were about three Australians with us.

"Think about it this way, if you're going to lose somebody, who are you going to lose first? Right, the guy with the least training and experience. Yeah, get rid of him and go on. Later on, the same thing happened. This is what happened. Second convoy, same camp. They said, 'Armijo, and so and so is going on the choppers.' They checked me out. 'Do you know how to launch a grenade launcher?'

"'Yeah.'

"'OK, test that thing.'

"'One, two.' I had two of them, and I had a whole bunch of grenades to go in the helicopter ... lead the convoy, check areas, and then come back with the convoy ... fly shotgun over them.

"We were *supposed* to go in the helicopter. Last minute, 'No helicopter. You just ride with the trucks.' So I'm going to ride with the trucks. The rest of the people are going to ride in the trucks. I'm supposed to ride in a helicopter but they tell me, 'Scratch that, no helicopter. You're going in there with the trucks.'

"So there's around two guys at the front of the truck driving -- Vietnamese. With Americans, but the Americans decide to sit in front of the truck. And I said, 'Bullshit.' They are riding *in* the cab with the Vietnamese. I say, 'No, I'm not going to do that.' So I sit at the back. There's around six trucks. We come up to a check point, Marine tanks join us and they move in close to us, hidden behind the convoy. We can hear them start up and start moving.

"The Marines are back there and we're around six trucks. We hit the same area. Fast. The tanks can't keep up with us but we know they're back there coming up in case we need them. And we hit the same area where they had told us before that we would get hit -- where I see that shell that was there -- same area. As we hit that same area, the Vietnamese in my truck start 'Craht, craht' -- you start hearing the chambers being cocked. And I *know* something's happening. The *Vietnamese knew* something's happening. I didn't know, the other . . . Oh, by this time, we've moved up the trucks far enough, and the tanks behind us, that another Vietnamese company joins us. And they say, 'Hey, everything's clear. Get in the trucks, and we're going gung-ho.'

"They are infantry and they get in the trucks because they've checked the roads. Everything's clear, so now we're taking off real fast. They didn't check it good enough. Because as soon as we hit the area, everybody starts cocking up their weapons. And sure enough, as soon as we hit that area, they hit my truck with a recoilless, we think it's a recoilless. The thing explodes, I jump out of the truck. Everybody jumps out of the truck. Those that could make it jump out of the truck.

"While you're jumping you're getting hit. The engine got hit. Later we left the truck there. It was no good. In fact, two or three of the Americans got blown away right there with the initial shot. Initially, there had been two Americans up there and then the other guys came up and joined us and got up on the outside of the doors.

"For a fact, I know they were walking around with no heads on. We get hit, we jump out of there . . . everybody's crying, yelling, everybody jumps out. But I remember back at the base after they told me I was not going to be in a chopper, I went in there and got grenades, grenades, grenades, grenades, grenades, and more bullets and more bullets, and a sergeant with me says, 'Hey, Armijo, you think you're going to a war or something? What the hell are you doing?' And I said, 'I dunno, I'm not gonna take any chances.' I didn't think I *said that*, I laughed it off.

"I remember that because when we got hit, and those guys were ... I'm here and those guys are out there . . . they're throwing grenades at us, they're making me jump all over the place. Grenades, they throw one grenade and I jump one way; grenades, and I'm jumping all over the place.

"They were VC. The guys up front, the guys that were left over -- I remember one Hawaiian or Indian guy, he had his legs shot somewhat. He was asking for grenades and I was passing them over to him. And he would throw them over the road. I was glad I had enough grenades to do that. But after a while I was the only guy left to shoot. Everybody else had got to gettin' -- there was people dead all over the place. And they're shooting, throwing grenades and we're not shootin' back except for me. After a while, my weapon jams, the M-16. And I'm playing, messing around with it, and taking a weapon away from a dead guy, trying to make it work. And this guy picks up his little funky face to see if we were dead, and just then it cocked, clicked, and BOOM! right in the face. I dunno if I killed 'im. He went down. I dunno if I killed 'im.

"There was enough of 'em to stop a full convoy. They made a kill, they made a kill. They came through. The idea is that they hit us, and that they roll over, they go right through 'ya. They tried to. But there was the Indian guy that was wounded and maybe a lieutenant that had some shrapnel in his face. They were alive but they weren't shootin'. So we decided to pull back. We pulled back.

"The tanks moved in and the tanks got wiped out. The Marines got wiped out. There was two tanks, they both got wiped out.

"The other trucks were behind us. We were the lead truck. When they stopped us they stopped the whole company. The trucks behind us were burned. The people were burned to death. If you've ever seen burnt bodies, that was the night . . . day to see 'em. They were just burnt. The thing exploded, or something exploded, and they were all just *charcoal*. Dead bodies.

"Right before we got to where we would have to go, before we got ambushed, we picked up a whole civilian load of people and put 'em in the trucks. After that we were stopped by the infantry company. *They* got on the trucks. So the trucks were *full of people*. When the thing started exploding, there was a lot of people in the trucks and a lot of them got burned alive.

"There's about four of us, five of us, from my truck. Four, five, that's it. A lot of them took off running, ok? A lot of them just run -- shhhooomm! You never see them again. But there was four or five of us . . .

"In our truck the people that were on fire were killed. Everybody else got shot to death. The truck behind us, they were all dead. I could see them. They were all burnt to death. People, you know, women, babies, soldiers, everybody burned. Laying on the road, dead.

"There was about two Vietnamese, the lieutenant . . . they killed two Americans in the initial shock. Two, that were out front. The lieutenant was alive, the Indian was alive, myself, I was alive. And maybe three Vietnamese at the greatest. But a lot of them got away because they just took off running through the bush. Some of them stayed with us but you could see them later on -- dead, next to me. Behind us was another truck -- who got away or what, I don't know. I just remember dead bodies. Burnt bodies.

"We're there, I'm shooting the damn M-16 like crazy. I'm just *feeling* that if I stop shooting, they're going to get up and rush at us. So I keep shooting -- any place. There was trees, at the trees, at the lower brush, any place I could figure out they were at -- I'd shoot.

"I had enough magazines. The problem was that the weapons would jam. We pulled back over maybe thirty feet and the lieutenant says, 'Stay there, we're going to move back here.' So they move back and I'm there looking at a little bit of brush this way with dead people on this side that had tried to crawl over, and they were dead now. And I'm lying there and pretty soon the brush starts moving. So I get up. I get up and run towards where the lieutenant was. He says, 'What the fuck are you doing here? I told you to move back!' He's not yelling, that was good on his part. 'What the fuck are you doing here?'

"I'm pointing. I'm not talking. I know they're there. I'm just pointing, 'They're there.' So I sit behind some trees. We had camouflaged outfits, and these guys, sure enough, come out of the brush. You *see* them live as shit. You know how GIs complain about never seeing the enemy? There are two of them. AKs, coming ... But they couldn't see me, and I wasn't about to tell 'em I was there.

"They didn't rush me. There was some dead bodies, they were picking up the weapons from the dead. They walked up maybe three feet away from me . . . and I unloaded . . . a complete, probably twenty-four bullet magazine in them. Dead people.

"I guess that's the only time . . . they were down, they were kneeling down, sort of trying to hide. They just stayed and DIED.

"No blood. Straight. BOOM. Just purple marks on their bodies. Purple. Dead bodies.

The Chaos of War

"What happened is that the A-Camp where we were going, sent out one or two companies. They came out in trucks. They met us, regrouped us, and we walked out. Helicopters came out and took out the dead. The South Vietnamese cut the ears and noses off the dead VC. I thought that was gross. I didn't like that shit. They cut their ears off, cut them off, cut their nose off. I looked at the Vietnamese, 'What the hell are you doing?'

"I didn't see Americans doing that. I saw some asshole trying to beat up on a prisoner. I didn't like that. 'What the fuck are you doing?' Troska, Troska, beating up on a . . . we were going up on a hill and somebody yelled, 'There they go!' We chased two guys up a hill, came down a hill. We couldn't find shit. We were following two farmers. 'You must be VC!' He started interrogatin' them. The fucker didn't speak Vietnamese so anyway he started beatin' the shit out of them, just to make them talk. I didn't like that shit. I told him, 'I don't like that shit.'

"I'm thinking about the same camp that was surrounded by an NVA company ... battalion ... whatever it was. Here in the mountain, they hit the camp and then they moved in across the river. They're attacking it, so they bring me from Da Nang into camp to go reinforce this friendly company trying to hit that (enemy) battalion. The battalion of North Vietnamese had moved across the river and they're hitting the camp. Then we come in with a company to hit them. They bring me in from Da Nang.

"They bring me in on a chopper. We get briefed on what's going on. We're going to take in more supplies, and I'm supposed to drop in too. So the helicopter takes us there ... it's a matter of minutes, ok? Tuhh, tuhh, tuhh! It comes down, and I'm coming down, and I'm kicking the supplies over from the chopper, and the colonel says, 'Your turn. Jump!'

"I didn't jump. I said, 'I *can't* do it.'

"He said, 'Jump!' We were maybe two stories, no parachute, no anything, just jump. We were gettin' hit, alright? The choppers coming in were gettin' hit. He says, 'Jump, jump.' I says, 'Uh, uh! I'm not jumping!'

"To me it was too far down. Not so much the shootin', as just the height. The chopper has to pull out, they drop me back off at the camp. I'm supposed to join them *somehow*. The colonel didn't give me a lot of shit about it. He was pretty good about it. He knew it was hell. He knew it was shit.

"I think after you've had combat experience you don't do the same dumb things.

The Joking Stopped

"Other times it was just walking up and down hills, looking for action. Actually, killing people. If we had to, we would just call in artillery--all night. You're afraid of lights moving down there so you call artillery all night.

"We didn't have snipers in the usual sense. We got shot at ... but more like an ongoing battle.

"We often weren't in a position to snipe at anybody because Americans are too noisy. Our LRRPs were for recon, not for sniping. Snipers to you is I'm here at A-camp and I want to send one guy out there to see what he can find. To them, it's different. For one thing they're not approaching the same type of fight you're looking for. *You're looking for a competition. They're just looking to make you weak, a little bit.*

"You come in with big choppers, you come in with big tanks, you come in with big troops, with big, noisy backpacks and all this bullshit--all I have to do is wait for you and at least get one of you down, and move on. That's all they want. What do you want? You want to confront them and destroy them; that was our main objective. To find them and destroy them.

"Sure, we could have fought the war more successfully without the noisy line units--but only if there were no North Vietnamese. North Vietnamese moved in like battalions. They wanted confrontation ... at their opportune time. You know, you're talking about what if we had only sent Special Forces and maybe Rangers to do the guerrilla warfare? Fine! If you're dealing with the VC. Shit, by the time we were moving in there, I think we had guys, confrontations, with an organized army! I mean, they weren't going to take any shit from you.

"That time they were cornered in there like I was telling 'ya. Here's the hill, and these guys are moving towards the hill, and we move in there with jets, helicopters, gas--*they didn't budge*. They just didn't budge enough. They waited till nightfall and they just kicked our ass out of there!

"That was no longer any sniper fire. They were well trained. See, they wouldn't have pushed us back had we all been Americans. But ... we had Vietnamese there. Maybe they didn't have the discipline. The NVA moved us back that night and I joined them the next day.

"One of our A-camps, Cu Duc, I can't remember the name, had a landing strip. It was out there in the hills. Again, an Australian sergeant said, 'Recheck this area here ...' So I checked out the area. I had to go up a trail and find a house. The map showed a house. I had two or three Vietnamese. I walked up there. We got close enough to something, then the Vietnamese **FROZE**. And they got down on their knees, down like this (to create a smaller target). And I was standing up, I couldn't understand what was going on. [Editor's note: The Vietnamese sensed an ambush, or otherwise dangerous situation.]

"With the little experience that I had, I came back and I told the sergeant, 'I couldn't find it.' So we came back. About a month later, that place was taken over by North Vietnamese. And they were around us--I didn't see them. But they were there. They just came up on that camp and cleaned up on the Americal.

"But what I'm saying, we had a landing strip, we had around a full battalion there, and they got wiped out. In one afternoon. Oh, no, no! The Americal was there. They came in to reinforce us, and *they* got wiped out. They got wiped out. I guess what I'm saying is it was no longer sniper fire. This is just plain all out war out there.

It's beautiful country. That was beautiful. We walked into some trails where we found the old French machinery for straightening out the roads. You know, they had the wording in French and all the stuff there.

"To me that didn't make sense. It was a highway. The highway was sort of ... closed up. And the machinery was there but I didn't ... But that highway probably led up all the way to Ho Chi Minh or whatever. I looked at the trail and I found some stuff up there but I couldn't find the house and these guys didn't want to move.

"They sensed something, something that me, El Paso, naive, doesn't know shit about. Thank God they didn't want to move anymore.

"I actually got the Bronze Star after the ambush of the convoy. That changed things a little bit. The joking stopped. The guys became a little bit more serious.

"That was interesting. To me it was interesting because I'd never experienced that before in my life. And I didn't know what in the hell was going on. I'm getting shot at, and around two days later I make it back into camp at Da Nang. And I was there and the colonel comes up to me, 'Where's Armijo?'

"'He's out there some place.' Sergeant Major runs out there looking for me. Sergeant Major was, you know, a professional. He runs in, 'Armijo, colonel wants to talk to 'ya. Right NOW! Look at yourself and sort of straighten up your shirt, and whatever else. You run out there.'

"The Colonel, Chango, I think it's Chango. I don't know the exact spelling. I get confused, one was a colonel and one was a major. And he says, 'Fuck, what the fuck were you doing out there, Armijo?' Very serious. This was after the first ambush when the two guys got killed. Very serious. I did not know how to respond to him. He just said, 'Good job' and shook my hand. I saluted him.

"Actually, nobody was killed in the first ambush. The two Australians went on patrol and were killed later. Nobody was killed in the first ambush.

"The colonel just smiled, shook my hand and says, 'Tomorrow afternoon, three o'clock, fifteen hundred hours, you're going to be awarded the Bronze Star. Be there.'

"He says, 'Bronze Star' and I say 'What the fuck is this guy talking about?' So I walk back in there to our headquarters. Everybody's talking about me. This and that, that and that. What happened? How did you do this, and how did you do that? You need to get your debriefing. They wanted to know why I had done it, how I did it ... I couldn't tell them. I said, 'I don't know. The trucks were going through a trail, there was a big ...' They wanted me to give them a logical A, B, C and I couldn't do it, so finally they said, 'Ok, show up here' and they read a big statement as to what I had done, a two-page statement. I guess that's where I get my ideas as to what happened.

We're Winning the War?

"I used to read that shit about how we were winning the war. Bullshit! Bullshit! How many North Vietnamese they had killed in I Corps. Bullshit! I guess from the fact that we were gettin' our ass kicked all over the place. That's what happened. I don't know what it was. But if you have an A-Team at Cu Duc, or whatever, I'm trying to remember, with the American supporting us and *they* get wiped out and we're still winning the war? Then Phum Duc, and they come down the mountain, and I was sittin' there, and we hit 'em with B-52s and I could see the song--have you ever heard a song of B-52s? Bzzzz, bzzzz, bzzzz, bzzzz--all the beautiful music before the bombs hit the ground. It's a beautiful noise. Bzzz, bzzz, bzzz, bzzzzz. Then everything just starts going Brrom, brrrom, brrrroooom. Cleans out the whole thing. Then *five minutes later*--kuchacoo, kuchacoo, kuchacoo, with the same mortar. We didn't kill the fucker! He was still there!

"I just saw it (the B-52 bombing) this one time and I never want to see it again. It's terrible! That whole music, that whole mountain comes down! That thing shakes, rattles.

"Or you hear the Navy shootin' inland. That's terrible, too. Big, big gun. Whatever it is. Boom, phoorum, PHOOOSHH! The *whole earth shakes*. I was in I Corps, but they were shootin' even close to us. They would blow all over the place, just shake the ground.

"Khe Sahn, our camp, got wiped out. We were at Thon Duc, I keep calling it Phon Duc. We set a perimeter this way along the river, thinking they would cross the river this way. And until today I think it couldn't have been the North Vietnamese, it couldn't have been the VC. But they started hittin' us with BIG, BIG, BIG GUNS. Phoom, phroom, but they were hittin' the river so it wasn't really hittin' the ground to the point where it would hit you and knock you over. But I'm not kiddin' you, the water was splashing into my face and I was in a foxhole. And I was the only guy down there close to the river.

"I had to think I was cool. I was a young kid. The other guys would go up and sit up close to the banks ... and do their thing. I would go over there and sit with the troops, I was one of the troops (the Vietnamese). It would hit the water, splash the water, then shake the whole damn thing. For around five minutes we're going back and forth and I'm on the damn thing (radio), and I think it's Marines. That's the only artillery around there. 'Get those fuckin' Marines off our backs! They're killing us!' I'm yelling, I'm screaming, I'm mad and I'm tellin' 'em every ... That thing went on for five minutes before it stopped. Nobody ever said who it was. I'm assuming it was the Marines. God, that's terrible. THAT IS TERRIBLE. To get that incoming--big guns--you're not talking mortars. You're talking about a howitzer, or bigger.

"I wasn't so green by then because they kept sending me out with different companies. After the first time around, I was accepted. Nobody ever said, 'You don't have Special Forces training.' They didn't say that. One time I did get my ass chewed out. That time we were gettin' hit with the howitzers close to the river, the sergeant came up and said, 'Looks like it's going to be rough tonight or this morning. What are you going to do if the shit hits the fan?'

"'That way.'

"'Fuck! Do you have a compass?'

"'No.'

"He said, 'It's that way!'

"If we got overrun we had to go the other way. And I was looking at the river. And I thought I had climbed up the river this way. He said, 'No. Go the other way, you dumb shit.' He sort of was questioning whether I knew what the fuck I was doing.

"To him it wasn't a big deal. He was just an asshole sergeant.

The Waste of War

"One thing that to me is interesting is that those two bodies were healthy bodies. When you think of VC as being scraggly little guys--these guys had arms on them that you could tell they'd been moving around in the jungle for a long time. Big legs, big arms, just *husky* looking little fuckers.

"Yeah, I feel sorry about that now. I don't like it. I don't like the idea of guns ... shooting people ... stupid.

"You don't forget it (the war) and I think it's coming back to me by way of my kid wanting guns in the house. Play guns, baby guns. And .22s or whatever. I said *bullshit*! Guns are for killing, that's the only reason you have a gun. Don't give me this shit about target practicing. That's bullshit.

"People talk about needing guns in the real world. What is reality? TV? That's where they learn this shit. What's there to say that he has to learn to use a weapon against somebody? Either inside his house or in an army-type of a situation?

"I don't want my boy to learn to think he's a hot-shot and he knows something about weapons. I don't want him to walk up to me like a lot of kids walk up to you on the sidewalk and say, 'Bang, bang!'. I hate that shit, some kid telling me he's going to kill my ass!

"We're being trained. Society trains you a lot of times. They have TV, they have Reagan speaking, they have all this other bullshit telling people that they should go out there and act smart or act tough. I don't think it's necessary.

"My brother stresses the same point other people make, 'Hey, wait a minute! You're gonna make him into a pacifist!'

"So what? You know, so what? Pacifist versus an aggressive person who wants to kill. I don't know, I have a problem with it. We have all kinds of idiots here. I would read you a hundred reports here in this court, in this office, right now (Editor's note: Sergio was an attorney at this time. Later he became a judge.). Everybody's trying to kick everybody else out. And it's stupid.

"This talk of the Jews resisting violence with violence in Germany, could they have resisted? Could they have resisted against the Nazis? If it comes down to the preservation of your life, you're going to react.

"My wife is a farmer. And I go back there and they all have guns. And they see a little bird, 'Tweet, tweet, tweet, tweet'--'Look! This gun works!'--'KOOOSH!' And they shoot the shit out of the bird! What kind of shit is that? I disagree with all that shit. If they can shoot a bird, why can't they shoot a human body ... a human being?

"Let's hope they (my kids) make it. It's been my greatest fear that they won't make it. I hope they make it. It's three little kids, right, hope they make it. I hope they go through life. *Without going through war, without going through racism.* Maybe I'm asking for too much ... you hope for the best.

The Vietnamese Ate Rice, I Ate Rice

"I don't think I thought about things then like I do now. It's after you get out that you start seeing all this shit in perspective. 'Why did I isolate myself? Why couldn't I be just another GI? I saw people as just being people not just gooks. I treated them as people as much as I could.

"Like those two VC that I killed, they were just people. They fucked up, but they were just people.

"I don't believe in that shit of the survival of the fittest. For one thing, I would put up my three years wages as a soldier on the Vietnamese versus the Americans. They knew what they were doing. We didn't. We didn't know what the fuck we were doing.

"Simple point: We would go up the hill. We knew we would have to go up for three days, four days, and then go this way, go that way, and then come back, some shit like that. They would all take their canned food, their sleeping tents, and all this shit on their backs. And if they couldn't carry it, they asked a Vietnamese to carry it for them.

"I took my rice. The Vietnamese ate rice, I ate rice. It was soft, it wasn't heavy on my back. I didn't take no sleeping tent, no bullshit; I knew I was gonna sleep on the ground. I would take out my poncho and just lay it on the ground, and just lay on top of it. These guys would take all kinds of shit, and be tired and bitchin' about it.

"They didn't impress me as being super tough. They'd get tired, they'd scream, they cried; we'd be going up a hill full of leeches, they (leeches) crawl up your ass and all this shit and these guys would be crying. Ahhhh! And the fuckin' Vietnamese would be laughing at them! I think in their minds, we were not sensitized to their environment.

"I just did what was the easiest to do to survive. You had to stay light, as light as you can. We didn't wear the tin helmets, we wore the cloth hats. Very few carried the entrenching tool. I never took that shit with me. I remember some guys diggin' some foxholes and telling me, 'Get in there tonight' and I would do it just in case something happened.

"I remember gettin' lost. I remember taking a platoon with me and their saying, 'We're going up this way, we're going to be here'--and I hit the elephant grass and pretty soon I was *over there!*

"I don't think I would do it again. EVER. Unless they were in my backyard, then I might have to do something.

"I would give up the experience I had in Vietnam, but only if I could have the same experience without doing it. (Laughter) Without puttin' my ass on the line! I think it would be the nice way of doing it!

"I see that my life is no better than anybody else's. By the stroke of luck I'm here.

"We were training some Montagnards, and we took them across a little swamp that was dirty--and I remember because I got fungus out of that. I got fungus on my ankles. For about two or three months I wouldn't walk. But, by the stroke of luck--we were being shown how to approach a hill, or how to attack, or how to do this or how to do that--and I was gettin' off the rock this way to do something and I was going to step this way and the guy in front of me stepped--blew himself up on a land mine. Yeah. By the stroke of luck. It could have been me."

Chapter Six

Tanks and Beetles

1967
4th Infantry Division

H. Bert Maltos

"Every day we kept returning to our base a little bit later than before until we got caught coming back at night." Bert Maltos

Riding The Taxi
Smoke in the Tank!
The Fucked Up Wounded
The Cracker Box

Riding The Taxi

"It amazed me how electrical a tank was. And how roomy! It moved around as if it was really light even though it was heavy. It had a top speed of maybe 40 miles per hour.

"I learned really fast to never put my left leg in the way of the barrel when it was going to recoil. The loader would load and I would fire and feel the recoil. I had a six-inch clearance.

"We had a young, nineteen-year-old lieutenant who was resented by the Lifers. We operated out of the 4th Division Headquarters in Pleiku in the Central Highlands. I remember kids running alongside the tanks during my first convoy and thinking, *This is a trip. I can't believe this, I'm 10,000 miles away from home!*

"Others didn't have that attitude. We had a kid named French who was a likable lout, profane, got high, always smoking dope and drinking. He would scream at the kids, 'Get out of my way, you fucking gooks!' Then he would try to run over the chickens and dogs with the tank.

"People were probably safer in APCs (Armored Personnel Carriers) because they could escape if it was hit and burning up. In a tank, only the driver could escape out through his hatch. The rest of us had to go out through the turret.

"It surprised me to hear the veterans say that it was safer outside. They always slept on top.

"One company had about 20 vehicles (tanks and APCs) and would escort truck convoys north and south of Pleiku. Quite often, we would take convoys north to Dak To about 30 miles. Twice we escorted 30 deuce and a halves carrying ammo and fuel. There were no trees, no brush beside the road. The mountains were bare and you could see for miles. They had grunts guarding the trucks, two of them per vehicle.

"On occasion we would come across them coming in from the field. They would talk to us on the radio, 'We're just 400 meters down the road' and so forth. Then when we would see them they would razz us, 'You guys've got it easy riding in a taxi.'

"We would see them and they would have a week's growth of beard and long hair. One of them said he hadn't had a bath in 43 days. I found out from a friend later that what they meant was that they hadn't had a full bath in that time. But every time they came to a stream they would clean up some.

"We would spend some time back at headquarters between running convoys. There was this other Chicano, a guy from Santa Fe, New Mexico, a Spec 5 who was a cook and also drove the jeep for the 1st sergeant. He looked like Luis Gamboa back home, except he was taller and darker. He had a large nose and jet black, wavy hair, a mustache and glasses. This guy had a 'Fuck the Army' attitude and was always insulting the Lifers.

"A couple of times he tore into this poor Lifer, a nice guy really, who had been in for twelve years. He would say to him, 'How come you're in the Army? How can you stand this shit?'

"As I said earlier, our commanding officer was this young lieutenant, a kid really. The E-6 Lifers really resented having to call this kid 'Sir'. This lieutenant really wanted to prove himself, to get into some action. We would go on convoys or on patrol and stick to the roads and hardly ever see any infantry because they didn't like to be near the roads. Every day we kept returning to our base a little bit later than before until we got caught coming back at night. The troops were grumbling that, 'One night we're going to get hit.'

"There were four of us in the tank, I doubled as a gunner and medic. We had French who ran over chickens and was the driver and a loader and we had the lieutenant. There were 12 tanks and one APC.

Smoke in the Tank!

"It was dark outside and we were coming back from town. The battle of Dak To was raging in the far hills and suddenly the driver yells, 'Goddamn it, Charlie's out there. Let's get the hell out of here. Let's start shooting!'

"I got hit on the left side. It burned. I twisted, writhed in pain. Then we got hit on the right and everything exploded and I got some shrapnel. I was scared.

"I knew I couldn't get out, the lieutenant was above me in the way. I couldn't reach the turret. It was dark in there; it was suddenly a small cubicle, no longer roomy and modern. They were shooting at you with B-40 rockets and recoilless rifles. We had been able to see the explosions and flares and tracers in the hills where the Battle of Dak To was raging, but now it was here right around us. A group of VC (Viet Cong) had sneaked around and attacked us.

"They were shooting at you, there was smoke in the tank, it was filling up with the acrid odor of fuel burning, and flames menaced in the corners. There was terror, plain fright. If I could have run and panicked, maybe I would have, but I controlled myself.

"I was bleeding, a rocket had come in, shearing the tank's armor plating, and torn off a piece of my hip and rear end. I was bleeding, wounded for 45 minutes before the Dustoff (Medevac helicopter) came in. The whole time I was firing away, terrified but desperate. We used up all the ammo we had, maybe 10,000 rounds of ammo. We fired white phosphorus, commonly called Willy Peter and heat rounds. They were huge shotgun blasts, thousands of darts.

"We'd say, '45 degrees left, longitudinal left, 35 degrees right.'

"We were leaking oil, on fire. We thought the tank would blow up. Can you imagine the tight compressed space in the tank filling with black, gagging smoke and the terror of the fire reaching the fuel systems? And we couldn't run, had to keep firing.

"Finally the Dustoff came to get me, but I lay on top of the tank on a stretcher for a long time. I remember saying, 'Boy, you sure have one hell of a hole in your ass!'

"Even while I was being lifted off I could hear the staccato of the machine guns and could see the tracers cutting through the night.

"They asked me while I was on my stomach on top of the tank if I wanted morphine and I said, 'No, it doesn't hurt now.'

"'It'll hurt later,' they said, so they gave me an injection. I didn't have a chest or stomach wound so there was no danger that the morphine would slow down my respiratory system. My heart would not stop.

"Later the lieutenant told me we'd put flares out so we could see the VC. We'd shoot one and another would come and drag the first one away with meat hooks. That way we wouldn't know how many we had killed. The lieutenant himself got wounded in the legs at the same time I got hit.

The Fucked Up Wounded

"They flew me to Pleiku to the 91t Evacuation Hospital. I was there for three days. While I was there I couldn't see very well because I had lost my glasses when I got wounded. A marine had killed an NVA prisoner right when I got there. It freaked me out. I didn't know what to do.

"They sent all ambulatory patients to Tokyo, Japan. I spent 45 days in Japan, getting operated on in Yokohama, getting the skin grafts from my legs and thighs to put on my butt.

"I was never put under. They gave me local anesthetics to deaden all feeling from the waist down. They gave me a spinal injection.

"Two doctors worked on me, one that reminded me of the 'Fugitive', a Dr. Kimble from Chicago who was about 5 foot 10 inches tall, a white guy in his late thirties with a full head of hair.

"The other doctor was pudgy, had a beer gut and a flat top hair cut.

"The nurses were young women, very attractive ones. The head nurse was a first lieutenant who wore a starched, white dress and was tall and slender.

"For quite a while I was sore. The aching would make me grouchy. I had been told to lie still on my belly but I couldn't stand it any longer so I got up and walked over to where the other ambulatory were sitting watching TV. They caught me and sent me back to bed and the graft didn't take so they had to work on me again.

"During this time I still didn't have my glasses and had to squint to see anything.

"I had been put on the 6th floor of a huge hospital. There were a lot of wards. On my ward you could tell who the Marines were. They were fucked up, the wounded; there were lots of wounded Marines--they had their legs and arms blown off. This Marine of about 20 years old had barely been in-country three months when he caught some shrapnel in his stomach. He told me he remembered his 'gunny' (gunnery sergeant) had got wounded, had stepped on a mine and lost both legs. It really hurt him to know he would no longer have the same 'Mr. America' physique. This gunny had really prided himself in having a beautiful body.

"Lots of guys in my ward had to have their intestines removed. A part of their intestine would be sticking out and the shit would go into a bag. There would be all these Marines running around with bags for their shit.

"Only one guy freaked out. I saw his face in the paper in September of 1970. It was the Yakima paper. His name was Charlie Smith (pseudonym). He was from the Detroit area and had been sent to Chicago after the war. The captain had told us he'd lost both legs but now he was walking down the aisle to marry his nurse. He walked on artificial legs to marry the nurse who had taken care of him. It blew my mind to pick up the Yakima Herald and see that same face again.

"I was in a state of disbelief when I saw his face. A lot of things were going through my mind then. I wasn't bitter then, I was rather proud. I had been sent home to Madigan General Hospital outside of Tacoma in Fort Lewis. I was there for six weeks.

"I was happy to be flying home to the States. We wore blue pajamas when we flew from Japan to Madigan; it was a neat feeling but yet it was also sad because everybody was splitting up; when you were the one who had to stay, you would watch all these guys leave and when it came time for you to go, you knew exactly how it felt to stay behind.

The Cracker Box

"They had intended to keep me in Japan longer because of the skin grafts but after six weeks I protested and they finally sent me to Madigan. The Army sent me to my present company where I stayed the last 20 months of my Army hitch.

"It was a bad enough wound. I could walk, but not well enough to be sent back to Vietnam. Probably, I could have gotten out on a medical discharge if I had really pressed it enough, but I didn't know any better.

"This is when I started to become disillusioned. During the last 20 months, it got to be really bad. The vets were disillusioned, we were subjected to a lot of stateside Mickey Mouse shit and harassed about haircuts, brass, starched fatigues, you name it. Overseas, this crap wasn't stressed and quite naturally, we didn't like to have to do it now.

"I went on leave to Mabton to see my parents and friends. I had written to them to not worry that it wasn't that bad, but they kept insisting that I sit down, that I not walk so much. And I could understand it.

"Back at the base, I was assigned to 551st Medical Ambulance Company. I drove a cracker box, a square-shaped vehicle with a red cross on the side. It was 1940 vintage with a stretcher in the back, really nothing to brag about. They assigned us to a Basic Training company and I attended all their PT tests, their bivouacs and we went along with them to the rifle range. Most of the time, we sat in the ambulance and watched.

"Some of the other guys harassed the trainees, but I didn't take part in that. But I did think the trainees were babied. When we had gone through Basic Training, a truck followed our marches and picked you up if you were badly blistered. There was no first aid, no ambulance. It was all topsy-turvy when we got back. All these kids that were being drafted had to do was write Mom and they would come down with a big investigation. The veterans didn't get any respect from the Army. My God, we had been in Vietnam, and they still made us pull KP! I pulled KP when I had barely 35 days left in the Army. I resented this so much, I wrote "35 days short" on my white cook's cap and infuriated the E-6 Black mess sergeant. 'What the hell do you think you're doing in my mess hall?' he screamed.

"But the guys that were coming in to eat cheered me when they saw it and said things like, 'You lucky dog, we wish we were getting out.'

"Pulling KP, scraping the slop from the dishes and all that crap, was with you wherever you were. I pulled KP in Cam Ranh Bay when a bunch of us first came in-country. When we first got there we had three days to wait until we got our orders about where in Vietnam we were going to go. So the Lifers got you to pull KP and other shit details. Finally, on the third day, they lined us up and these Lifers got up behind their podiums. They started calling out names, and you were supposed to go to these dozen or so white stakes they had stuck in the ground. You line up behind them when they called your names. It went something like this: 'Jones, Jim, Pfc, serial number xxxxx, 4th Infantry Division, move off to xx stake.'

"Finally, they called my name and I found out I was going to Pleiku. When I got there, they put me on a shit burning detail. It was a 'sanitation' detail. I was a medic, right?

"Both at Cam Ranh Bay and Pleiku, we had to burn the shit in these barrels. A mixture of gas and diesel got thrown on the shit and they ignited it with toilet tissue. It gagged you to have to smell that shit. It seemed like every Army base had its skies blackened with those black clouds of diesel and shit smoke. That was a lot of what being in the Army was all about. It was gross. After the flame went out, you had to go in there and scrape the barrels clean. Then you took everything and buried it or threw dirt over it.

"I remember taking a crap over one of those barrels. You'd sit down, putting one cheek on each board, and looking down, almost gag. There among the turds and slime, would be the flies and maggots and beetles. These 2-inch bugs, called Goliath beetles, would be there swimming in the shit, their shiny coats were visible. We used to watch them when we burned the shit. We would pour the diesel fuel on them and watch them trying to get away. But there was no way out. What a way to die!"

Chapter Seven

Like the Fourth of July

H. Bert Maltos

4th Infantry Division
Medic
1967

"The tank is on fire, smoke billowing out, and we couldn't move foreward or backwards." Bert Maltos

Running a Convoy
Morphine
By Plane to Japan
Good Wounds, Bad Wounds
So He Went Home

Running a Convoy

Anyway, the unit I was in kept coming back later each night until we finally got ambushed. The ambush was part of a larger battle of Dak To that was taking place. I remember telling the lieutenant that it was a bad idea to keep going out for supplies and coming back after dark.

If I remember right, the Battle of Dak To lasted a month or so. I told the lieutenant, "This is a bad habit that we're getting into, going out early for supplies and waiting until it's dark and going back out towards our base camp." And I told him, "We're going to get hit one day, and sure enough that's what happened. We were in a convoy. Running in a convoy, all we were doing was protecting them and hauling supplies back and forth. That was basically that we were assigned to do.

After I was wounded a helicopter came in and picked me up. They put you on a stretcher or sling and picked you up. It was still dark outside. It was at night, it was dark. I was conscious the whole time. I think the firefight lasted a good forty-five minutes but it seemed like ... just ... well, it seemed a lot longer.

In the beginning of the battle. What triggered it? We just suddenly got hit. Suddenly--BLAM-- we got hit. The first shell penetrated the bank because I was in the very first tank. Just a wild guess, I'd guess there were a good twenty tanks or APCs, a good mixture of them.

You would think there would be a lot of wounded all along the column, but as a matter of fact, from what I can remember, there were only two of us, just me and the lieutenant. There were two wounded in the first tank, but nobody was killed. I was in the very first tank and they hit us in a cross-fire. They hit the first tank and the very last one. They did that to stop the column. From what I can recall we were hit twice, two shells ... from both sides. I can't recall if the very first one hit me or the second one, but anyway I remember one coming in at about face level. I was sitting on a gunner's chair because we were one man short so I was doubling as a gunner and medic on the lead tank.

It was pitch dark inside, it was night-time, and when the shrapnel fragments came in it was like the Fourth of July -- very reminiscent of the Fourth of July -- with exploding fireworks inside the tank, and very loud, almost psychedelic, in a way. And then the other shot came through and I knew I was hit right away (when that one came through). I could feel it hit me -- kind of like a burning sensation. I remember reaching down and patting myself on my rear end and I came up with a bloody hand so I knew I was wounded. My pants literally were on fire -- they were smoking.

Like I said last night, there was a sort of panic, which is understandable ... hysteria. The tank is on fire, smoke billowing out, and we couldn't move foreward or backwards. But luckily we still had power enough to turn the turret so we were able to use up basically all of the ammo. But we couldn't move the actual tank backwards or forwards; we were stuck there. Fortunately we could move the turret and shoot.

The lieutenant could probably see where the fire was coming from because he was the tank commander. He could probably see the sparks or the flame -- on occasion -- where the fire was coming from and direct your return fire there. He was the one that could do that because, of course, he had had his head out of the main hatch with the binoculars. So, yeah, he was directing the fire.

When I was hit I thought -- maybe not consciously, but . . . or maybe it was conscious but I didn't . . . didn't verbalize it. I didn't say it out loud, but you thought of . . . Mom . . . at that instant ... I did. I really did. It was . . . an instinctive thing. I really thought I was going to die. For sure. I was really scared. We all were, but me especially because I was the youngest guy in the tank. Also, the driver was pretty hysterical. He wasn't hit, he was just scared. Very scared. 'Cause he was up front all by himself. You know how the drivers are, the location, in the little hatch up there. Anyway he was really scared, screaming and yelling.

He had nothing to do because he couldn't move. He was pinned, really. I can understand. He probably wanted to get out and run. I know I did, that's for sure. I *would've*, I have to be honest, if I would've been able to get up and run, the way I felt, I would have because I was scared. I just wanted out of there.

They called in a Dustoff medevac after they had shot some flares to illuminate the area where the enemy was. I think it did last about forty-five minutes but it seemed a lot longer.

Morphine

Anyway, the Dustoff finally came and they thought they were going to lift me out but I said, "No, I can pull myself out. I can help you guys." I got out and they put me on a stretcher. Another medic from another tank came by and checked me out and put an ABD pad on my ... ABD is short for abdominal pad which they use for wounds in the abdomen. They're just big, huge pieces of gauze. It was a big wound. He asked me if I wanted morphine and I said, "No. Believe it or not, it doesn't bother me right now. It's not hurting me."

He said, "You better take it. Right now, yeah, it might not bother you. But later on you're going to feel the pain, so you'd better take it."

I said "OK" so he gave it to me in my thigh, intramuscular. That's the best way to do it. It's more effective that way. Right through the pants. Do you know what those morphine shots look like? I could tell you a little bit about them. It's just like a miniature tube of toothpaste. It has a little point, it's almost like a superglue container, you break the tip (it's a glass tip or plastic tip), you make a hole in it and you squeeze it out like a little tube of toothpaste. You stick it in somebody's thigh . . . and squeeze it. That's what it is. It's morphine. It's supposed to be given intramuscular either in the thigh or the rear end or shoulder. It's in a liquid form.

I did not feel high right away. Not that I could tell, I really didn't feel high. Maybe because I was excited. I mean, my adrenalin was flowing, pumping because I was really excited.

The chopper landed right next to the tank. They put me inside and they took off. That was the first time ever, in my life, I had been on a helicopter ride.

I don't know if they made any efforts to get our tank out of the way, to push it out of the way. I'm not sure. I don't know, but I think they were just concerned with checking and making sure everyone was okay and keep firing away. Because by the time the chopper did come in and they put me in it and we were taking off, it was kind of dying down . . . the last few minutes, sporadic shooting here and there.

So they flew me to Pleiku. I'm gonna back up a little bit and talk about my Mom, that she had a premonition, a sixth sense, sort of, when that happened. She told me, not too long ago, I would say . . . what, maybe four or five years ago, or maybe not even that, about that, that she heard me say, "Mom!" And I was amazed and I thought, "You know something, I did say that." Because I'm sure I didn't mention it, what happened, exactly, and she told me, "All I know is that day, November twenty-second, 1967, the day it happened, I was doing the laundry or something. I was by myself in the house, I know I heard your voice or I really feel like I heard your voice and I could tell you were in trouble because you yelled my name . . . 'Mom' . . . in an urgent fashion."

And I was amazed. I said, "I did. I'm pretty sure I did say that." You know I *was* scared. I believe her because she has experienced other things in our family that lead me to believe that she really does feel . . . that she really does have psychic abilities, if you want to call it that. For example, four or five years ago one of my older cousins died of cancer. This woman, her name was Tina, lived in Dallas and she was one of the daughters of my mom's oldest sister. Tina and my mom were close to the same age, they were only, at the most, five years apart, so they were more like sisters rather than aunt and niece because they grew up together.

Anyway, my mom had this premonition -- what, maybe days or a week before we found out that Tina had died, my mom had a premonition that Tina was sick or that something was seriously wrong. So my mom wrote a letter and mailed it one day, and we got a phone call the next morning, real early in the morning -- 5:30, 6:30 -- the bad news, "Tina passed away of cancer." My mom was really all emotional, upset, of course, and she said . . . she started telling me, I remember this, "I *knew* there was something wrong with Tina. I just had this *feeling*, something was wrong with Tina."

Anyway, she went back to the Post Office and told the story to them -- "Hey, could I have this letter retrieved? Give it back to me please because I just found out my niece just passed away of cancer. You know, I had addressed this letter to her." The Post Master said, "No problem, I understand." He gave the letter back to her.

But, that's just one example. I could tell you more. I think my mom is psychic, or something . . .

I really don't remember whether there were any other choppers; all they had to do was pick me up. It was dark and hard to tell. That chopper might have been the only one, because if you recall . . . those choppers had probably been flying over Dak To all during the day and maybe the night. It was standard procedure for those choppers to have a gunner or somebody with a weapon. I think, if I remember right, that was the only chopper, there were no other ones around. The lieutenant, I think he did the patriotic thing, he was gung-ho, really gung-ho, he stuck around. They picked him up later on because he wasn't that badly hurt, he had shrapnel, a few holes in his legs, in his calves. But it wasn't that serious. So I think he hung around and they picked him up later on.

I don't think the lieutenant's wounds were that bad. Not as bad as mine. I definitely got out of the country after that. I don't think he was hurt that bad, no.

By Plane to Japan

I spent three days in Pleiku, 91st Evac Hospital. I remember the first thing -- you know, I was conscious all during this time -- when I was taken off the stretcher and put on this cot or operating table, right away they descended on me like a horde of vultures (chuckles), men and women both, majors and captains most of them . . . drafted doctors. They literally stripped me naked, tore off my clothes and one of the first things they did was stick an IV solution in my vein, you know, one of those bottles, to replace the liquids I might have lost.

Being a medic, was I aware of what it was they were doing? Yes, I had an idea. I had served in a hospital, but I was just a glorified pill pusher.

They flipped me over on your stomach and put a pad on my rear end. Luckily I wasn't bleeding that much because a person's rear end is mostly fatty tissue. There are not many veins and I wasn't losing that much blood.

I guess I was kind of lucky to get hit there. I spent three days in the hospital there and then they shipped me to Yokohama, Japan, the 106th General Hospital. After I was in Pleiku for three days they shipped me and a bunch of other guys by plane to Japan.

One day a doctor came in and said you're going to Japan. Oh, one interesting thing when I was there those three days in the 91st Evac Hospital at Pleiku -- they took everything away from me, they took my glasses and so I couldn't see very well, but I could see well enough that thirty feet away was an armed MP (Military Policeman) and I remember asking the Corpsman or one of the other patients, "Hey, what's going on there, I can't see, I'm near-sighted. I see there's a guy over there, an MP." They replied, "Oh, there's an NVA (North Vietnamese Army regular, the enemy) over there."

So there was a wounded NVA soldier being guarded, twenty or thirty feet from my bunk. And the MP was there not to stop him from killing us, but because (I heard from some of the other people) a couple of days before, somebody, one of the other patients, had tried to cut that guy's throat. One of the other GIs, a Marine, had tried to cut the NVA's throat so they put an MP to prevent it.

Stories you heard about doctors cooperating with interrogation teams, injecting mercury into wounded prisoners, I don't know if they were true or not because they do take the Hippocratic Oath. I wouldn't say it's not true or it's impossible. I would say anything is possible. Nothing shocks me anymore . . . whatever I find out about the Vietnam War. I wouldn't doubt it. (A shrug)

Anyway, there was an NVA soldier there, a wounded patient, being guarded there, day and night, around the clock by various sentries . . . eight-hour shifts. Isn't that something? (Pause) I spent six weeks in Japan as what you call an "ambulatory patient". I don't remember much of the plane ride out of Vietnam to Japan.

I was not put on a litter and carried out. I walked out, because I was classified as "ambulatory" -- I was able to move on my own power. I moved slowly, of course. I was sore, in pain. They helped me up the ramp. I don't remember much of the plane ride out of Vietnam to Japan, but I do remember vividly the chopper ride once we got to Tokyo. It was a brief half-hour ride once we got to Japan, and I remember looking down like a little kid, all of us, looking down on the freeway -- and it was exciting.

I still didn't have my glasses, but I could see halfway clearly. Anyway, I spent six weeks in Japan. I was ambulatory, so I was able to get around, walk around. I was able to talk to some of the patients. You could always tell who the Marines were. They were the most fucked up. Always, without a doubt. Guys with no arms, no legs -- it was pathetic. I remember talking to this one guy, Sullivan. Irish, right? Good-looking guy, a twenty year old kid, from Boston. He stepped on a landmine, a Marine, right? Both legs were blown off. One was blown off below the knee and one was blown off just above the knee. On one leg, what was left of one leg, on a thigh, there was a chunk of meat missing. His arm was in a cast, it was in one of those casts where you're not supposed to move, because it was shattered with shrapnel. His arm was all torn up. I think that was basically it.

He was on the same floor, the same ward. That hospital had something like eight floors and each floor was called a ward. We were in the same ward. I remember talking to him a little bit, and I thought to myself, *That guy's ruined for life.* Twenty years old.

What did he say? He was still in some sort of shock. Kind of in a daze. Probably on drugs for pain. You better believe it. So maybe that's why he was kind of in a daze. Not believing this actually happened. But also on drugs to kill the pain.

Good Wounds, Bad Wounds

I talked to various people, but the people I talked to, basically, were the . . . patients. Not much to doctors or nurses.

We talked about how we got wounded, how we got hurt. I remember talking to this one guy from Mississippi. He was a staff sergeant, a twenty-year old staff sergeant. Battle-field promotion . . . . 'cause the other guys were killed, so he was promoted. I remember him telling me -- I think he had been in -- country eight months before he got wounded -- that he was very happy . . . to be going home. Anyway, he was telling me some of the things he did. Like he remembers killing this old man, wasting him; he had an

M-60 and he blew him away. He was laughing when he was talking to me about this. You know, it didn't really bother him, you could tell it was nothing, he just . . .

They had gone over the line, a lot of those guys . . . I guess. He just killed an old gook. It's no big deal. He said a few other things.

He was Army . . . Infantry. Twenty-year old staff sergeant . . . from Mississippi . . . a good 'ol boy.

How did he get wounded? I'm not sure. I think it might have been a grenade or mortar round exploding close by, because just by looking at him walking around, he wasn't hurt that bad. He was one of the lucky ones.

He got wounded in a strategic place so they were going to send him home. But just by looking at him, he didn't look that bad at all.

(Pause)

There was also a black guy, an Army guy, who was shot in the face. It was strange how his face was swollen like he had been in a fight -- grotesquely swollen -- because the bullet had gone in through one cheek and had come out and broken his jaw. He was also going to be going home later on. I remember he and I were talking and you know how -- you're well aware of this, how the common usage for the medics was 'doc' -- so he was calling me 'doc', and he said something like, "Doc, you know you're lucky, you didn't get hurt that bad." You know, he was saying stuff like, "Look at me, I got shot in the face."

I just listened to him. I didn't really say anything. By the looks of his face, he didn't look like he needed plastic surgery. Once the swelling would go down, I think he'd be okay. He could grow a beard over the scar.

Let's see, who else can I think of? Oh, the most important: Charlie Smith [pseudonym]. This was very poignant, pathetic, whatever you want to call it. There was this guy named Charlie Smith. Again, another young kid, twenty years old. He was combat infantry, Army, and he had -- here again -- stepped on a mine, both legs blown off, his balls were lost, shrapnel in his guts, his intestines. I think he lost a couple of fingers on one hand . . .

He was on drugs to kill the pain. I felt sorry for the guy. I think everybody in the ward felt sorry for him because . . . It was very sad because at night the guy -- almost nightly, almost every night -- he would cry. *Literally*, he would cry most of the night, and we all heard it. And I felt so sorry for him, I thought *Jeezus!*

A young, white kid. I think he was from Michigan, the Midwest somewhere. As a matter of fact, I've got a newspaper clipping of that guy in my apartment in Seattle and I'll bring it one of these days. He was the one who married the nurse! Yes! He walked down the aisle on artificial limbs, on crutches! He is the guy, I know he is! Charlie Smith, 'cause when I cut *that* little paper out -- it's got a picture of his face, too -- I know that's him. How many Charlie Smith's were double amputees? That's got to be the guy I was with in the hospital.

It might be that a lot of Vietnam veterans in hospitals just stayed there. You know, what I always wonder about is . . . after any war . . . you just don't see that many amputees or veterans that lost their ... Maybe because we live in a small town, I don't know. But you don't see a lot of amputees walking around or guys in wheel chairs. When you do see a guy in a wheelchair you find out it was an auto accident, you know what I mean?

I think maybe the greater majority of Vietnam veteran amputees are located in big cities. Or near hospitals, big cities, big metropolitan areas where they can continue to get assistance. Yes, maybe that's why you don't see very many around here. There are quite a number of veterans that are wounded, but they are people that can function . . . walk around. Most of the people we see have both arms and legs. It's a curious point.

(Pause)

In Japan I killed time by talking to people, listening to the radio, walking around because I *was* ambulatory although for a while after they operated on me and put skin grafts on my rear-end; and they told me to stay off my feet and let it heal. I was a fool, so antsy, frustrated and bored, that I deliberately walked around, and I remember doing this one day: walking around to where the TV was, even though I was near-sighted and still didn't have my glasses. But I squinted and sat in front of the TV and I remember one of the other patients telling me, "God, hey, the doctor told you you should be in bed." Eventually I did go back to bed and lay in bed. But by doing that, walking around and so forth, I ruined the skin graft -- it didn't take. So they had to operate on me again, and the second time, it took.

What they did is they took skin from my legs. Like I said, the first time it failed because I didn't follow orders. I was walking around when I should have been lying there on my stomach and relaxing. But the second time around, once they took more skin from me, I thought I'd better do what the doctor says. So I did, I lay in bed, and this one took. The doctors would periodically go through the ward and check out each patient, and they said, "Good, this one looks like it's taking."

No, I didn't see any young nurses fall in love with their patients, but yes, the nurses over there were young. Most of them were young, and they were attractive. But most of them were officers, lieutenants and captains, and we were all enlisted personnel. They must have had another hospital for the officers, because all the people that were there were E-6 and below. No, 1st Sergeants and below, and as far as I know there weren't any officers there.

1st Sergeant were E-8's. Yes, I pretty sure they must have separated the officers from enlisted personnel. Even in death, you're separated. Ironic, isn't it?

I'm not sure if the Army notified my parents or if they told me to. I do remember writing a letter from the hospital and more or less just telling Mom and Dad, "Hey, I don't want you to worry. I got wounded, but I'm going to be fine, don't worry."

To a certain degree you could look out the window into the city. You could look over the buildings. Yes. The hospital was towards the outskirts of town. To get to Tokyo, you had to get on this subway, or a train, like in Brooklyn, commuting between suburbs. Once the skin graft took and they did classify me as ambulatory, I was able to sweet-talk the nurse, a first lieutenant, into giving me a 24-hour pass. I convinced one of the medical corpsmen, a nineteen-year-old kid just like me (we became friends, in a way) -- to go with me to go to Tokyo. Like I said, I conned the nurse into letting me go. She said, "Ok, ok. Here's the pass, I'll give you permission."

So we went and we boarded the subway that took us into Tokyo. We walked around and stuff.

We didn't buy any tea or anything, but we went to a little bar where we took off our shoes, kneeled on a cushion, and had some saki. We were the only non-Japanese people in that little bar. But they were very nice.

The medical corpsman knew his way around a little bit because he *had* been stationed there in the hospital for a while. There was nobody to talk to so we became friends, sort of. (Pause) I kind of wish, now, that I would have gotten that guy's address. Who knows, maybe twenty years later we could have gotten together. "Hey, remember me?" "Yeah!" Curious. I never did. I can't remember what his name was.

So He Went Home

I can't remember exactly how long after we went to Tokyo on that pass, but I was in Japan six weeks. Then I was asked where I wanted to be stationed, and my first choice was Fort Lewis over here in Tacoma and the second choice was Fort Ord, California. The third choice was Germany. Luckily, I got Fort Lewis.

I was sent to Fort Lewis, and actually, I could have gotten out on a medical discharge if I would have faked it. But I was real honest and I completed my three year hitch. I was sent to Fort Lewis and I was assigned to this medical ambulance company as a truck driver. I was here for my last twenty months, almost two years, before I got released. I was walking by the time I got back to Seattle, or Fort Lewis. I came back with the other wounded. The ones who were severely wounded were going home, they were getting medical discharges. Others, like me, who weren't that bad off, we were going to our next duty stations.

(Pause)

For twenty months at Fort Lewis, I was just a babysitter, really. That's all we did, we went out with the Basic Trainees and followed them in our "cracker boxes"--those ambulances like you've seen in MASH, with the big red cross on it.

During those twenty months I was able to get weekend passes and so forth. As long as I wasn't on duty on weekends. I would go home to Mabton on weekend passes. I mostly came home to see my parents. At that time I didn't know Richard Gamboa, or other friends I got to know later.. Who would I see? -- Basically I just came home. At that time I didn't know Rico. I didn't know Sixto, I didn't know you, wow . . . basically I just came home. I didn't even go to the bars because I wasn't quite old enough until my very last year in the service. Yeah, isn't that ironic? So I just came home to see my parents, basically. The drinking age was twenty-one. So isn't that something? I just came home to see my parents -- basically. That's it. Because all these people that you and I talked about, Rico, and Richard Gamboa, and you and Sixto, I didn't know any of you guys at that time, in '68 and '69. And I wasn't quite old enough to drink until January of '69, when I turned twenty one.

I didn't go back to back to school until the fall quarter of '72. September. GI Bill, all the way.

What caused me to go back to school? Boredom. I wasn't doing anything there at the house in Mabton. Why did I go to the University of Washington in Seattle? I was recruited by a fellow Mabton alumnus, Raul Anaya. You know, one time he saw me there drinking coffee at the Mabton Cafe. He started talking to me and told me, "You know, I've been working with the University of Washington, Schmitz Hall, in minority recruitment."

He graduated from Mabton, Class of '67, one year after me and he talked to me and I thought, "I'll give it a try, sure, why not?" Because I was bored. All I was doing was drinking a lot. After I got out of the service I was drinking a lot and doing menial jobs -- field labor -- and just wasting time and whatever and I was feeling very anxious and depressed and, you know, I really felt like I was wasting my time.

This was a couple of years after I'd gotten out. Because I got out in . . . '69. Yes, it was three years later that I went to school. I wasn't aware of any other veterans going back to school. I *swear*, as far as I know I think I was the only Chicano veteran that I *knew* of going to school at that time, in 1972. (Editor's note: In fact, Lionel Guerra and Jimmy Sandoval, both combat veterans, were at UW at that approximate time, but Bert wasn't aware of this. Probably others, too.)

In my hometown of Mabton? Yes, I ran into Jim Godinez (a pseudonym) when he was *crazy*. He was a Marine who returned from Vietnam. He was AWOL (Absent Without Leave), and I think they finally gave him a bad conduct discharge when they finally caught him after deserting, or whatever. The reason why Jim Godinez went AWOL, and I don't blame him, is because, like a fool -- after his first tour of duty in Vietnam, he extended. So he went home on leave, and while he was home on leave, he decided, "I'm not going to go back." Anyway, he deserted or went AWOL and they finally caught up with him and gave him . . . I'm pretty sure he had a bad conduct discharge, or a general; I'm pretty sure it's not honorable.

He's crazy. There is something wrong with that guy, he was affected by Vietnam, really. Yes, I mean he's crazy in a *wild* sort of way. Well, because of the experiences that he saw, that he went through. I mean, he was either in Khe Sahn or Con Thien.

Chapter Eight

With My Men in the Bush
A Hispanic Infantry Officer

Robert E. Sanchez

1966-67 Combat Tour
1969-70 Adviser

"Even when we went to sleep at night, a little noise, leaves falling from the trees, would cause my eyes to automatically come open . . ."
Robert E. Sanchez

Recon Platoon
Those Are Bullets!
Mines on the Road
Losses
Pleiku
Transition
Firefights in the Trees
Like a Candy Store
Hispanics
A Hardening Process
Advisor in the Delta
Hoa Hao
Guest of Honor
After Vietnam

Recon Platoon

"I was a lieutenant operating out of Tuy Hoa on the coast. One day command decided it was going to change its method of operations and sent me and another man to LRRP (Long Range Reconnaissance Patrol, pronounced Lurp) Training at Nha Trang. The Special Forces ran the school so it was pretty decent. The only problem was that they only trained two of us and didn't give us time to train the men. I wanted to have the men themselves sent to the same school, but that was overruled.

Lt. Robert Sanchez (later Captain) led a Recon Unit (LRRP) in Tuy Hoa Province, South Vietnam.

"The Battalion CO simply said, 'You are now the Recon Platoon. We want you to go out as a squad, set up ambushes, stay behind to catch the enemy trying to sneak up on us, etc.'

"The only training I had time to give the men, if you want to call it that, was basically to say to them, 'You'll be the pacer out in front; you, the second man, cover the pacer; you two men cover the sides; and you, the drag, cover our rear.' It was very basic and really incredibly inadequate. I got back from Recon School and went with my men right into the bush. I had absolutely no time to train them.

"Our patrols were lonely affairs, just a few of us out there in the brush. If we were ever discovered by Charles (the Viet Cong), we would have been in a world of hurt. Generally, we would throw off the VC by staging a lot of phony landings. The choppers would go in low next to a zone that was appraised to be safe for one reason or another or they would saturate an area with artillery, then go in with choppers. If only one ship had made a landing, Charles would have known where we were and would have done a number on us. But the decoy landings worked.

"After landing, we would move according to our sense of things, sometimes to a sixth sense. We would move very slowly if we sensed an ambush situation, and we would conceal ourselves really well at night. Sometimes we would go really deep into the brush or tules and wait. The mosquitoes would eat us raw, but at least we were safe. We would wake up all mottled with bites on our hands and faces.

"At other times we would sense that we were being surrounded. Either we saw something suspicious crossing a trail or a spotter plane warned us of the enemy trying to encircle us, and we would throw caution to the wind and get the hell out of the area. In circumstances like that you were in more danger by going slow than by gunning your engine and scrambling out of there. The times when GIs stepped on booby traps were not in times of flight but during routine patrols when someone didn't look closely enough for signs of a string or trip wire. I was on a mission like this when we heard it over the radio that one of my men had been blown away in another sector.

"As a LRRP you're constantly in a high-risk situation. Even when we went to sleep at night, a little noise, leaves falling from the trees, would cause my eyes to automatically come open and I would remain that way, super-tensed, for a period of time until I was satisfied that it wasn't someone trying to sneak in on us.

"You're constantly on a tight-rope, you're treated differently. In our case it wasn't as much so as in others because they weren't trying to treat us different other than the missions they gave us. In other words, when we were back at base camp they wanted to treat us just like common infantrymen. They wanted to give us the same details even though we were on call where we could go out literally any time. The company, on the other hand, was also on call in a sense; they would go out if another unit got hit, but for us it wouldn't have to be an emergency. It could be just that someone had a mission for us. They'd say, 'We want you to get us some reconnaissance or we want you to set up an ambush, or we want you to go in with a unit. Get ready! You're going!'

"With a company, it wasn't that way. You got so much time in which you could count on being back at base camp. So obviously, you had to maintain the discipline. But with a LRRP unit, this sort of thing was not as essential because the discipline is either there or you die. It's not the type of situation where you had to worry about discipline breaking down at base came because it would affect the discipline out in the field. The LRRP knew that they couldn't afford that, so they had to maintain their discipline.

"We spent a lot of time out there in the bush by ourselves. It was cold and miserable at night and it rained a lot all of the time. As soon as the rain stopped, the mosquitoes came out in swarms. The men were suffering from jungle rot so bad, some of them had to be medevac'd out.

"The colonel didn't seem to give a damn about us. Not a plugged nickel. We were out there God knows how long to where our skin was shriveled and spotted and we wanted to come in out of the bush 'cause of the jungle rot that was eating the men's feet. We at least wanted some more support. We asked for another team to be sent in to replace us but the colonel said no.

"It was a frightening situation to discover enemy activity all around you and to ask for help and be refused. But we knew there was another company of GIs in the area so we began moving towards it. We asked for permission to join that company but that was refused by command. You have to realize that the men were at the end of their rope physically and mentally and weren't getting any support. We kept moving towards that company. We never traveled down a trail, always across it. We were moving in file through this growth when I stopped and called out to one of my men to hold it up. I later learned that that was the only reason a GI ambush party had not pulled the trigger on us, thinking we were the enemy. Up till then they had been tensed up, listening, sitting behind their machineguns and claymore mines thinking we were an NVA unit trying to move in on them.

"I stopped my men and hollered, 'Don't shoot, we're friendlies.' Then we set up next to them for the night. I don't imagine the colonel was overjoyed, but the men had been ready to cash it all in. They were just about eaten up by mosquitoes."

Those Are Bullets!

"We went out to a sand bar on the coast to check for enemy activity. Sampans had been sighted going to the sand bar and we had reason to believe VC might be in the area. A stream of tracers, machinegun fire, came in over our heads while we paddled our little rubber boat over to the sand bar. At times the bullets hit close enough to splash water on the men. I asked the RTO (communications man) to get on the radio and ask them to stop, assuming it was probably our own men. We told them the firing was coming from over the ridge. This told us it was undirected fire, not hostile fire. Headquarters replied that there was no firing going on. We insisted that there was firing coming in from over the ridge and that they were coming perilously close to killing us and would they check it out on the double. This while the bullets bounced and skidded around our rubber raft.

"The radio operator came back in a melancholy tone and assured us there was no friendly activity going on and no hostile fire had been detected. Finally, I took the radio and hollered into the transmitter, 'Look, I don't want to argue with you. The shells are splashing us with water.' I stretched out the transmitter, 'Can you hear that? Those are bullets!' I let it sink in for a half a second. 'Just send out a gunship over the ridge quick!' They complied and shortly after the firing died down.

'Earlier, the same had occurred when M-50 fire had come in over a patrol. It had been a U.S. Cav unit out practicing. Another time, our patrol got caught in the open by hostile fire and called in a gunship which did fire on an enemy gun position.

"These rubber rafts didn't offer much protection, even if you went out at night."

Mines on the Road

"One time, this hill was being hit. The VC were throwing everything they had at it. We got the call on the radio, so I rounded up some APCs (armored personnel carriers) and jeeps and headed up there. This all happened on the coast near Tuy Hoa. Well, the lead APC hit a mine and got knocked over. We went on and got to the hill and picked up the wounded. We were going back and the medevac APC that was loaded down with the injured hit a mine--it must have been electronically detonated because we had already been over the same road. It started burning. We tried to pull the guys out. It was hard to get close to the flames and we thought it might blow up. One of the guys had his straps hooked in somehow and we couldn't get him loose. We had to slash it with a knife. He was screaming and looked like a burned pig, bloated, horrible. We were helpless to help him. It was terrible. Just terrible beyond description.

"The guys on the hill must have gotten lax and the VC hit them.

"Even if we had been reinforcing by chopper, we still had to have somebody there to signal us in. So it was six of one and half a dozen of the other whether to come in a track column or by chopper. They both entailed certain risks. A lot of places in Vietnam, particularly the Tuy Hoa area, had a lot of rice paddies. We had an incident where one of the PCs hit what looked like a hole in one of the rice paddies, flipped completely over and sank out of sight.

"We had some people trapped down there that were eventually able to get out. It wasn't safe to cut across rice paddies; and I don't think it was something that we wanted to be doing anyway ... going through their rice paddies ... because this was part of their crop, their livelihood.

"You had experiences in Vietnam when you were exposed, either necessarily or unnecessarily, to danger. During the incident in which the APC was blown off the road, I was riding in a jeep and felt a little exposed. But you've got to go. There are times when you're exposed, when you're moving down a trail or checking out this village or hamlet. That's why you have the cover tactics, why you advance some men while the others provide cover. Obviously, the people that are advancing -- if somebody decides to open up on them -- that's part of the time they're exposed. You know that there's that danger but you've got to go ... you've got to go. You're just hoping that you've taken enough precautions so that if something does happen, you will have the advantage even though you may suffer some casualties.

"This type of combat experience was very different from the sporadic terrorism that occurred in a city like Saigon. Terrorism in Saigon or any other city was a lot like a car accident, it didn't mean a whole lot unless you're involved. It didn't mean a lot unless somebody was constantly driving at you, trying to get you involved. Then it meant something. If something happened down the road, you could say, 'Well, there was a crash down there.'

"Terrorism was an impersonal type of thing because nobody is saying, 'I'm going to get that guy.' It wasn't as personal as when you got out in the field and you were actually hunting one another. *Then* it became personal."

Losses

"In Vietnam, you got to know people quickly. I lost a couple of people from the Long Range Reconnaissance Patrol Platoon. One of them hit a mine, and I guess I didn't completely lose him because he did recover eventually. I imagine he did make it back to the states. Then I did lose another one that was sniped and killed. We were out on another patrol when we heard the transmission. Those were the only two I lost as a member of the LRRP Platoon.

"As a member of the rifle platoon, I lost some people. I think the *only* people I lost were due to our own friendly artillery. I didn't lose any people that were killed as a result of action. I had people wounded, but not killed.

"It's difficult to gauge what kind of impact a death had on buddies. I know that as a platoon leader, you lose men but you really can't dwell on it because you've got to keep the platoon going. You feel sorry that you lost someone but you've got to have them replaced and continue on the mission. Otherwise you might end up losing more.

"So you can't dwell on it. I'm sure that it had a bigger impact on people that had spent a lot of time together on the same squad, the same team. Not necessarily only that they had lost some friends, but also that they had come so close to being dead instead of their buddy.

"As far as colleagues, I really didn't lose any over there. I had people that I had gone through Officer Candidate School with me that were over there. I had one that was in the same company; he's the one that was trapped underwater in the 'PC that turned over. He made it out, everyone got out, but I guess he had kind of been given up. But they did get him out.

"Also during one of the miscues by the artillery, he was one of the people that had several men who were killed. I watched the impact that it had on him. With him it was another close call. Yeah, he was concerned. He was concerned that it was getting close, that he had had some close calls. He wasn't sure that he was going to be making it out of Vietnam."

Pleiku

"After a while they transferred our battalion to the Pleiku area, away from the coast and into the Central Highlands. There were some immediate problems in this because the commander decided that we were going to continue to do things the way we had done them on the coast rather than the way that they were done around Pleiku. The seasoned chopper pilots couldn't believe it when we told them that the 4th Division was only going to use one helicopter to make the insertion of our recon units. The helicopter pilots were used to sending in one chopper to insert the squad, one to standby to pick up the squad in case the first one got shot down, and a third chopper, a gunship with miniguns, to cover the operation.

"It didn't make any difference that it was more dangerous in this area. The decision had been made to use only one ship. We would presumably outsmart the VC with decoy landings.

"I brought this all to the attention of the colonel, an asshole from Hawaii who didn't know his ass from a hole in the ground. This guy was small, not chunky like a native Hawaiian, but thin like an Anglo. The plea for reason, for more helicopters, went nowhere. The major backed up the colonel simply because he was the colonel, and the captain was kind of a buffer between me and the colonel. The other lieutenants didn't have to worry about this problem of the single helicopter insertion, or at least didn't have to answer to the colonel, because they didn't report directly to the battalion. They weren't the recon platoon for the battalion.

"When I was moving with the company later on, it was a totally different feeling because we had a lot more firepower, but you still had to be careful. In my case, I had to deal with the resistance I got from some of the older NCOs (non-commissioned officers) who may have thought I was a green lieutenant or maybe they didn't like Latinos. I learned that there were times in the bush when you didn't have time to explain why you wanted something done or why, in turn, you couldn't comply with a request. And if one of them simply stayed on top of you or otherwise harassed you, you simply told them to fuck off."

Transition

"When I transferred from the LRRPs to the company, I was experienced in terms of movement. I knew how to avoid the enemy during movement. I knew what to ask of point men, what to ask of the patrols going out, and what to check for in terms of our own perimeter.

"You felt more at ease with a large unit, but still when you were moving through enemy territory you felt a need to look at yourself as a small unit. You needed to look at yourself as a platoon or as a squad because you needed the same security in trying to avoid possible traps like following a trail and not taking the precautions that you would as a smaller unit, or taking off after someone who had fired on you and not being cautious enough to check for the possibility that you might be drawn into an ambush just chasing one person.

"In fact, we did have a situation where we did spot an enemy soldier in the Highlands when I was with the company. A couple of our men took off after him and chased him for a short distance. They gave up the chase and we kept moving. We didn't just drop everything we were doing to chase after somebody.

"No one that had been operating along the South China Sea, on the east coast of Vietnam, was an experienced infantryman when it came to operating in the Central Highlands. The Tuy Hoa area along the coast was principally an open area so during maneuvers we had known pretty much where people were.

"As LRRPs we had managed to stay hidden by moving at night, by using hedge rows and tree lines for cover, or by moving in with a company and staying behind. There were methods of stealth that we had utilized as a small unit that a company couldn't.

"During one firefight, the captain had set up two 90 millimeter recoilless rifles after we had received mortar fire. These weapons are carried like a bazooka, placed on the shoulder and fired. They made a swishing sound. After it was over we found two enemy bodies that had been turned into minced meat. They had hundreds of little darts everywhere in their bodies. The NVA had left a lot of empty foxholes behind when they retreated.

"When we set up, we would send out a recon patrol for a half hour, out about 300 yards. These were moving observation posts during daylight hours. At dark we sent out listening posts for detecting enemy activity. Well, in the early morning hours one of our patrols came in and said he had seen something.

"'Are you sure?' I asked.

"'Yes, sir. I'm certain.'

"So I told the captain about it and he gave me the same questioning look as I'd given my men at the initial report. I went out with a couple of men to check it out; this all while the company was getting ready for the day. We were walking through the trees when I saw them. They were crawling towards us, lots of NVA. I think we surprised them. I pointed and all three of us were pointing at the same time, then all hell broke loose. I emptied my clip as I turned to run. We burst through the perimeter and could hear GIs dropping into their foxholes. As soon as I got into mine I turned and fired tracers, then everybody fired.

"We called in arty and fighter bombers. We had the arty moving. If the NVA moved around our perimeter, we adjusted the arty and followed them. The battle lasted from around 6 a.m. to noon. All the while I crawled around from foxhole to foxhole, making sure the men had plenty of ammo and that they had the support they needed. The NVA had been sitting still, they had dug in during the night before moving forward. They knew more or less where we were or they wouldn't have been crawling toward us. Once we called in arty and TAC (Tactical Air Control) air, they began maneuvering under cover of the trees. They would also make diversionary attacks to try to draw us off so they could hit us at a lightly defended area. It was the captain's job to ensure an overall defensive perimeter, but he had suffered a shrapnel wound to the head during the attack and was not totally in command.

"As I said, the captain was wounded, but I don't know exactly when. I know I had gone back to him; I think I was trying to get more ammunition for my platoon because we were running low. When I had gone back there, I think he was already bandaged up because he had received some shrapnel through his helmet. I don't recall exactly what he might have said; I do know I went around to the other platoons and got more ammunition.

"The other platoons really weren't receiving any fire. In fact, during the whole firefight, it was just my platoon and another platoon that received any fire.

"We were in triple-canopy jungle, so there wasn't a whole lot of need to have a large perimeter. We were on the edge of a clearing but set up among the trees. We got hit from the triple canopy on two sides. The platoons away from the main approach of the enemy hardly got any fire. One platoon didn't even have to fire at the enemy. One of the platoons did have a Listening Post out beyond the clear area and lost their radio-telephone operator. In fact, they lost another man trying to go out to get the radio.

"We were set up among the trees and had all kinds of cover. Normally, we had the habit of clearing lanes outside of the perimeter. Inside of the perimeter, we left it pretty much the way it was. The captain was set up close to the center. We had quite a bit of cover, so inside the perimeter we could dash from tree to tree. We felt our cover was pretty adequate even though we did have people wounded. The mortar rounds that came in were falling among the trees. We found several that had not exploded.

"During the engagement, one of the men, a Southern hillbilly, told me he could see an NVA. 'He's over there by the bushes, sir,' he said. 'Watch this.' He took very little aim, it was a very deliberate but very quick burst. This guy had grown up hunting down in Kentucky somewhere. He fired and the bushes began to shake where he had hit the enemy soldier. The arty did its job too. Later we heard the explosions going on around us and thought they were grenade bursts, but we discovered later that they had been mortar shells. Finally, the enemy broke and we began to follow. We found NVA hats and equipment and blood trails. We had killed 24 of them.

"After the firefight, we broke camp and began to exit the area. We knew the cousins of the NVA, the Viet Cong guerrillas, would come around to pick through the trash of the rich American troops, so we burned what we couldn't take with us."

Like a Candy Store

"On another occasion, we decided to leave the enemy something to pick through. We wired some trash and a couple of trails with explosives and left five men for an ambush. They didn't have too long to wait. Two VC showed up, and walked right up to a couple of boxes as if they were in a candy store. That's how confident they were. They started to walk off and heard the click of the grenades. The one with the box dropped it and started to run but the wire wound tight like a snake around his ankle. He was killed by the explosion. The other one ran in the opposite direction and into our medic who was waiting with his M-16. 'I decided I had to let him go or save my life,' the medic told us, 'so I shot him.'

"We set up in the Highlands and called in marking rounds to establish our perimeter. That went well ... then they dropped several arty rounds inside our perimeter. They killed six people. Next time we set up we told them not to mark, but they dropped some more arty on us anyway.

"We were trying to sleep on top of our foxholes and suddenly I saw the red bursts over the tree tops. I rolled and called in to headquarters and yelled at them to stop. It turned out the arty guys had been drunk. That was really sad. One of our guys had been sick and had just gotten back with the company. It was really sad. Our own artillery killed him."

Hispanics

"I didn't find any clustering of Hispanics during my tour. Most of the Hispanics I met were able to communicate fairly well in English. As with any group, you're going to find enlisted men that don't feel comfortable with their Anglo peers. It's the same with any group, people are going to gravitate toward their own kind. However, I don't think you're going to find that within the officer groups because that's not the kind of training you get.

"I don't know whether I was treated well or not as an officer because I really don't have anything to compare it against. I don't know what caused the problems I did have, whether it was my lack of political know-how or tact, or whether I was perceived as someone who didn't have the necessary experience. I don't know whether any other junior officer would have had any different problems. The colonel during my tour in the field was Hawaiian and I don't know whether anyone who was not Hawaiian would have been able to communicate with him any better.

"My attitude toward joking along ethnic or racial lines has varied over the years. When I was stationed in Texas we used to joke amongst each other. We were well integrated there in terms of whites, blacks, and Hispanics. We were able to joke back and forth; I don't know to what extent the whites joked, whether they actually meant what they were saying rather than merely joking about it. I didn't know whether something that was light-hearted was taken that way or whether they took it to heart. It has always been difficult to tell. You really don't know.

"In Vietnam I never had any problems along those lines. Vietnam was a different situation; Vietnam was a life-threatening situation. If something along those lines was said in Vietnam, it was said in a serious fashion. The person probably needed to understand that it was going to be taken in a serious fashion. There could be serious consequences because it was nothing in Vietnam for somebody to get fragged because they didn't like him. He might get shot from behind if need be."

A Hardening Process

"After my combat tour in '66 and '67, the only problem I had when I got back to the states was dealing with petty things. In Vietnam you're dealing with a life and death situation and then you come back here and people are concerned because you don't visit them, and you're not proper, and maybe you're not as courteous as you should be. Their feelings are hurt. You begin to think 'What is this?'

"The other thing is that you're still on alert. For a time after you come back from a combat tour, every time you hear a car backfire or a fire cracker go off, you're looking around to see what you need to be doing in terms of ducking and so forth. Did somebody shoot? A lot of people probably don't understand this, that weapons fire takes on different sounds. Some of it can sound like a car backfiring, depending upon the distance. So you're never really sure as to what is going on. Is that a weapon? Or is that a car backfiring, or is it firecrackers--or what?

"Coming back after the combat tour was difficult even though I remained on a military base where I was training young men to soldier and to use weapons. It was still tough because we were back to playing games. We had to play games with scores at the end of the two-month Basic Training cycle. How high did your company score overall on the training? We were playing games with scores that didn't take a lot of variables into account, like how much education or initial motivation any group had."

Advisor in the Delta

"When I went back to Vietnam for my second tour in '69 and '70, it was because I received orders to go back. I know that there were some officers at Fort Lewis who had not even been to Vietnam for their first tour, and I was going back for my second tour. I wasn't even completely reintegrated into society when I got my orders to go back.

"I was going back as an advisor to the Vietnamese army. I flew in to Saigon and from Saigon we flew in to Can Tho, the capital of Ahn Ngan province, which is located in the Delta. It seemed like we spent three to four days waiting for somebody to find out that we were there so they could come after us. Finally they sent a jeep from Can Tho to take us to Long Xuyen, the district capital where I would spend my second tour.

"We were briefed at Long Xuyen and met the colonel. At first it was a headquarters assignment and eventually I was assigned as a district advisor."

Hoa Hao

"Not long after my arrival, I began to hear about a religious-military sect called the Hoa Hao. I heard that when the Vietnamese (government) had tried to organize militarily in Ahn Ngan province, the Hoa Hao had kicked them out militarily! The Saigon government had been trying to install South Vietnamese military officers to run the province and the Hoa Hao didn't go for that. I think they ended up with Hoa Hao in those posts.

"They must have been doing something right because Ahn Ngan was the most pacified province in Vietnam. While I was there, nothing occurred that would have led me to believe otherwise. There were encounters from time to time, but nothing that compared with anywhere else in Vietnam.

"I don't know if the degree of pacification was due to the Hoa Hao paying somebody off, whether they had strong ties so that nobody bothered them, or whether they were just in a situation where the VC couldn't get an infrastructure in there because the Hoa Hao were so strong.

"Like I said, I kept apprised of the military situation in my area, and I saw nothing in Ahn Ngan that compared with my combat experience at Tuy Hoa or Pleiku. As an advisor in the Delta, I was generally aware of the activity and involved myself in checking guard posts and the like. I would go out on the Baasaac River on our Boston whaler, a boat with twin-40 engines, a 16- or 17-footer with a square front. At times I also went up with Mr. Block, a warrant officer who flew our spotter plane. His job was to keep an eye out for unusual activity which occurred mostly on the waterways. He could direct counterfire on the enemy from his position, but usually it was a plane with miniguns that answered the call for assistance.

"Most of the violence that did take place occurred among non-Vietnamese, non-American third forces that were there to work construction or provide assistance of some sort. They would get drunk and sometimes shoot each other. We'd get a call that someone had gone berserk and shot a couple of people on a boat.

"The Baasaac River was patrolled by the Navy and it was the Navy that did the arresting if there was a need for that. The Navy also had a base in Long Xuyen and had a pretty good sized force there."

Lt. Robert Sanchez relaxing at a base camp. He doesn't drink or smoke at this point. See the note below

> To Mom & Dad and
> family.
>
> It may look as if
> I picked some vices, but
> it is all just a gag. I
> still don't smoke and don't
> Drink.
>
> I sincerley hope you
> like the picture. I will send
> another one in the future.
>
> Love,
> Bob

The Guest of Honor

"My views haven't changed much since I was there; I don't feel that we took seriously enough the cultural differences of the Vietnamese. We didn't respect the cultural differences enough. We wanted things to be done our way, regardless of what red tape the Vietnamese might have. Our attitude was 'This is the way it should be done.' This was primarily due to the fact that we were providing the aid. We felt that since we were providing the aid, then doggone it, things ought to be done the way we think things ought to be done. We had strings that we wanted to keep attached.

"So I think that a lot of Vietnamese felt that we were foreigners who weren't taking their feelings into consideration. They felt that we were trying to control them, to order them about, as if they were our lackeys. They were *resentful*. In fact, they cooperated a heck of a lot better when we would attend their activities, when we would accept some of their dress, or help them out in some of their projects. In fact, they invited us to their celebrations. They expected us to eat their food and to accept their offers.

"I ate quite a bit of their food. There were some Americans that would not eat the food there because they were afraid they would come down with some form of dysentery. And some did come down with some kind of bug. I didn't ever have any problems with the food, at least not that I could recognize.

"Most of the Vietnamese celebrations we attended were outdoor fetes. They were occasions where, for example, a mayor of a town would want to honor the National Guard that was coming into his area.

"The Vietnamese food consisted of a lot of green stuff, a lot of vegetables. Of course they had rice, pork, chicken, and mice. Mice were a common staple item; they would take small dogs to pinpoint the nest locations of the mice and then the Vietnamese would dig them out. They would pick them up with their fingers and put them in cages.

"You've got to remember that these were not disease-carrying rats; these were mice. They were grain-fed and were originally caught in the rice fields. They were for sale in the market place for anywhere from fifty cents to a dollar. They weren't cheap.

"I think they fixed the mice up for a meal by stripping the little pieces of meat off the bones. The chicken was prepared by chopping into tiny pieces, bone and all. Obviously, they removed the entrails. At times they'd save the head and serve it to the guest of honor. Of course, Major Guest (a ranking advisor) declined to eat the head. He said, 'Well, Dai Wee (captain), I'm not going to eat the head, you do it!'

"I said, '*You're* the guest of honor!' I can't remember which one of us ate it, but I know one of us ate it!

"They would prepare fish by wrapping it, entrails and all, and putting it in hot coals. Then they would 'bop' it and it would fall apart so you could see the insides of it. You would just strip the outside off it to eat.

"I don't think that we served any purpose in an advisory capacity, at least not where we were. I don't think that we ever got the people's confidence.

"I would occasionally wear the black outfit, the silk pajamas that the Vietnamese wore. So did my radio telephone operator and one other captain at his district. That was what the Vietnamese would wear; a Vietnamese district chief would wear his regular army uniform or his black uniform.

"It was somewhat unusual for a GI to go out to check the outposts at night dressed in the black garb. The Vietnamese would just smile. I think that they actually enjoyed the gesture. They appreciated that."

After Vietnam

"After completing my second tour I was assigned as advisor to a Reserve unit in Sioux City, Iowa. Not long after that I got my discharge papers. This caused me to become somewhat embittered at the military. They reduced their force by letting go of all the reserve people first before even considering the regular Army people regardless of what their record might have been. They said, 'All of the reservists are going first -- regardless.'

"I had earned my reserve commission before going to Vietnam on my two tours in '66 and '69. All of the people that had earned their commissions through OCS (Officer Candidate School) were reservists, and so they let us go. I don't know what a single individual could have done to effect a change in policy. But it does seem to me that they could have looked at the experience you gained during the war."

Chapter Nine

MP in Saigon

1966-67

Simon Carranza
U.S. Army Military Police

"Our job was to patrol the area between Saigon and Ton Son Nhut airfield. . . . We kept our lights on at night but only if we were in the city. Outside the city we used our dims." Simon Carranza

Buddhist Riots
Trial
Dong
Executions at the Hub
The Sailor
The Old Man Pissing
Black Market
One-Hundred P Alley
Haight Ashbury
The Chill After Saigon

Buddhist Riots

"When I first went to Saigon in June of '66, they were having the Buddhist Riots against the South Vietnamese government and even though we were MPs we were told to stay away. So we really didn't see a lot of the troubles of that period, but some of the old guys who had been there told us that two to three months before, the VC had run through the barricades at these officers' quarters with a pickup full of explosives. The MPs on duty reacted with shotguns and .45 automatic pistols but to no avail. This happened in Cholon, the Chinese District, and a lot of American officers were killed in that building.

"When I got to Vietnam I still had no deep personal feelings about the war. I remember how naive I was about the whole thing. In fact, in an orientation class when I first came in-country, this lieutenant had asked me if I knew who was the leader of Vietnam.

"I told him, 'I don't know. Hell, I don't even know why I'm over here.'

"He got mad and became abusive.

"'Beggin your pardon, sir,' I said to him, 'but you asked me a question and I gave you as honest an answer as I could.'

"As I said, when I went to Vietnam, I had no firm feelings about the war. Still, I was shocked and bothered by the thousands of little kids pan- handling in the street without any parents or food or place to stay at night. I gave them what little money I could so they could eat, but it still bothered me to see them on the street day in and day out, sleeping in the alleys, two or three of them together.

"Going in to the Army for me had been no big deal. Basic Training hadn't been all that rough because I liked to run, I was in shape. I had driven a truck before I went into the Army, a Browny with 3-gears, and generally I had been active. I got sent to Fort Ord but six of us were asked to take a Spanish test and we got behind schedule because of that test so they sent us to Fort Hood.

"When I went to Vietnam, I went to Long Binh, near Saigon, and was supposed to go to the field. Instead things got messed up and I ended up as a typist for 716th MPs. I didn't like it so I asked around to try to find another company where I could work outside. During this time I traveled around with a mail clerk and got to know the city pretty well. Finally I asked for a transfer to another company, to be with the same group I had been with in AIT (Advanced Individual Training). Right off it became apparent that I knew the city from having traveled with the mail clerk, and the new company didn't -- so I began patrolling for them. They equalized my extra duty by letting me off the hook on some other things. I had to show them all around.

"Our shifts went on for 8 hours, but we had to take extra time to get ready, to write our reports, and to clean our weapons. Sometimes after a shift or at lunch, I would go downtown and get us some Vienna sausage. I would get us some bread right out of the ovens. We would slap some butter on the warm bread and have us a real feast. That would be our meal, Vienna sausage, warm bread and butter, and a couple of cold beers if we could get them cold."

Trial

"As I stated, my paperwork was messed up when I got in-country, so I ended up as a clerk typist for a while. About this same time they were having a court-martial for this GI who had shot an ARVN (Army of the Republic of Vietnam, Vietnamese soldier), so I had to attend the trial as a court reporter. What had allegedly happened was that the MP, the GI, had been carrying a grease gun, which is a .45 caliber with an extended barrel and a wire stock. They said the ARVN had been sitting in a chair, maybe he was just having coffee, or maybe they were arguing, who knows? The MP had the grease gun slung over his shoulder, and he said that the weapon slipped and started to fall. He reached down to grab it but the jerking motion he made in reaching for it caused the round to go into the chamber and go off. It so happened that the barrel was pointed at the kid's head when it went off.

"The defense attorney was sharp. He convinced the jury of American military officers to acquit the GI. They acquitted him, but immediately transferred him out to the field. Whether it happened that way, I don't know. It's hard telling. A lot of those

ARVN guards would fall asleep on you when you were out on guard duty with them. The White Mice (Vietnamese civilian police) were known to fall asleep on you when you were two or three miles out of the main town. There would be nobody out there but you and that guard and whatever you were guarding. With two guys out there it would be your responsibility to poke each other to stay alert. But these guys would fall asleep so we would take their .38s or .45s, whatever they had with them, and give them to the duty officer that would come by. An hour or two later they'd wake up and wonder where their pistol was. We'd reply 'Didi mau'--long gone. A lot of them just didn't have the discipline, although some did."

Dong

"Dong, our maid, had four kids and had her mother living with her. She lived in a section of Saigon called Du Cau and at that time she was about thirty-five. She had about three or four rooms to clean and each room had about four or five guys. As a maid, her duties were to wash and starch the clothes, make the beds, polish our boots, and generally clean up.

"And to see her working with such determination to keep her kids going was really something. That's all she worked for. I'd ask her where her husband was. Sometimes I'd get no response. One time I asked her, 'Where husband?' That's how we talked. It was a combination of English and how the Vietnamese spoke it. So I said, 'Where husband?'

"'I don't know,' she told me. There was sadness in her voice but more a tone of resignation. 'One day he just disappear. Alive, dead, I don't know.' There was an interlude of silence, then she told me what I already knew, 'Sometime VC come take people away. They gone. Never see again. Fini.'

"I'd pay Dong a little bit more than what she charged. I met her youngest daughter. I believe she was eleven. She brought her to work one day. You know how you saw a lot of poverty over there, people in raggedy clothes. But her daughter always had her clothes real clean and she was very polite, very quiet. You could tell that there was a lot of love between the two of them.

"I witnessed close relationships develop between GIs and Vietnamese girls. A couple of MPs were actually living with young ladies. One of them had one child and the other one had two children. One of the young men was from Tacoma (Washington) and he was probably in his early twenties. I don't know whether he ever got her back to the States or not. He was having a hard time. He had left once and then came back again. How he managed to get back to the same area, I don't know. He did it somehow.

"But don't get the idea that being an MP in Saigon was all fun and games. Just seeing the orphans and the prostitution that people were forced into was painful. There was another side to it, too. Like the time an off-duty MP got rolled for his money. An American GI who had gone AWOL (Absent Without Leave) needed some money so he got this MP drunk and beat him up pretty bad and cut him up, too. Well, on a routine traffic check, other MPs stopped the AWOL and asked for his ID. The guy flashed the card he had taken off his victim and promptly got himself arrested. The MPs worked him over really good and didn't bother to take him to the hospital. The AWOL was white and the MPs were white, too."

Executions at the Hub

"When I first got to Saigon they used to take VC to the hub where all these streets came together. The Continental Hotel was in that area and so was the Congress building. They used to take VC to this other hotel to the east of the hub and execute them there. They had a sandbagged area where they shot them. They did it right there where everybody could see them.

"The feeling that comes back most often when I think about my tour over there is one of fear. Our job was to patrol the area between Saigon and Ton Son Nhut airfield. We patrolled Plantation Road and the Cholon area, the French cemetery, the race track, all of that. We kept our lights on at night but only if we were in the city. Outside the city we used our dims. On Plantation Road we used our lights unless there was some kind of alert.

"We spent a lot of time guarding the billets, the officer and NCO compounds, and those of U.S. civilians. There was a certain stress about a job where you are told to not let anybody who is carrying saddlebags on his motorscooter get close to you. The VC had been known to have claymore mines or plastic explosives with timers concealed inside those saddlebags. They would just set them down, then they would leave and you had to be real alert because those things would go off.

"I had one incident where a guy dropped a box near me. I yelled at him to stop but he took off running. There were too many people there, and you can't shoot innocent people. Why he dropped it, I don't know -- because there was nothing in the box. I got behind the concrete barricade.

"Another incident happened at night. A guy came riding up fast. I didn't pay too much attention to him. He threw the bike up against the wall -- it had saddlebags on it -- and he split around the corner. I called the duty officer. It turned out that it had a claymore in it. The bomb squad took it out."

The Sailor

"When I was there in '66 we used to go out to the Saigon River and this MP actually went skiing. He came back and his eyes were as big as platters. The VC had been shooting at him on the river as he went by on skis!

"Another funny incident happened when the Enterprise (aircraft carrier) docked near Saigon and unloaded thousands of sailors on shore leave. We had to try to keep them apart from the 101st Airborne Division troopers who also hit Saigon at the same time for R&R (Rest and Recuperation).

"I tried not to hassle the sailors; they had their own shore patrol on the docks, and we patrolled the city. The Navy guys were dressed in their whites and we were on foot patrol on Tu Do Street. This Navy guy seemed to be looking at magazines when we walked by. We could tell that he was drunk, but we kept going. Then we looked back and he was giving us the finger. 'I was just trying to ignore you,' I told him. 'You know it's past curfew, so why don't you go back to your area?'

"'I didn't know it was that late,' he said unevenly. I noticed he wasn't wearing a watch.

"'I lost it,' he explained.

"'How?'

"'Gambling.'

"'Do you have an ID?' I asked him. He fumbled around trying to reach into his own pockets. The entire time he was leaning against me so I grabbed him and gently leaned him against a black, wrought-iron fence. 'Stand right there. You're going to land on your face,' I said.

"I knew a shuttle bus was due any minute so I told him to get on it. 'If you come back,' I added, 'I'm going to take you in. If you stay out here somebody's going to hurt you in the condition you're in.' After seeing the cases that ended up in the hospital, I had no illusions about what the Bug-Eyes (street hoodlums) and the AWOLs would do to this poor sucker.

"He shrugged arrogantly and began to turn away from us to walk to the bus. 'I don't need you guys,' he sneered. We were taking this in as he continued turning and slowly we saw that his whites were perfectly crisscrossed with the patterns of the black grime where he'd been leaning on the lattice. We doubled up laughing.

"MPs didn't have it so bad getting girls. At curfew we would walk into a bar and holler, 'Everybody out!'

"Usually the whistle would clear everybody out. Then papa san would say, 'Can do, can do,' and we'd get the girls that they had."

The Old Man Pissing

"I was in a bus fill of MPs that came to a stop at a street corner. It happened that we stopped there when this old man, a real elderly Vietnamese, was taking a leak. Now, you've got to remember how Americans feel about somebody pissing in the street. You also have to remember that there were a lot of refugees from the countryside flooding into Saigon during the war. These people had different customs; it was normal for one of them to pull up his pajamas and hang his penis out to urinate.

"So when this elderly man did this, the dozens of GIs started pointing and laughing. The old man got flustered and pissed all over himself because he dropped his pajamas. Then the GIs really got to hollering."

Black Market

"There was a lot of Black Market activity in Saigon. The CID (Army investigators) would conduct most of the raids and we would go in as back-up. Most of the CID wore plain clothes and probably looked like civilians to other GIs. They lived in the same hotel where we lived. It was called the International Hotel on Trung Hung Dau, which was the main street between downtown Saigon and Cholon. We had all of our weapons and equipment right there at the hotel.

"One time at about three o'clock in the morning we were patrolling the streets and we came upon this motel and there was this Air Force guy outside with a young lady. There was also a White Mice, a policeman, there in civilian clothing. Evidently, the GI was shacking up or living with the policeman's girlfriend and the Vietnamese didn't like it so he came looking for him. He pulled a .38 caliber pistol on the GI. This happened on To Do Street. There was no way I was going to go for my weapon. If I did he was going to get me. He had all three of us covered.

"Finally by talking to him we got him to put it down. We had our hands on our weapons, but I was thinking, 'If I draw it, he's going to open up on us.'

"Fortunately, he understood a little English and we were able to convince him to put it down. We called in a back up unit, a jeep with MPs, and got the GI out of there."

One Hundred P Alley

"Others weren't so lucky. There was this place called One-Hundred P Alley, aptly named because you could buy any type of sex there for 100 piasters. At least, that was the word of mouth information that flowed around. But the true situation was that a lot of guys, especially Black people, ended up with their throats slit and their genitals in their mouths. It was bad news there. A lot of GIs found a way to get into that alley; it was actually a bunch of adobe buildings with a lot of lattice work made from bamboo. Some of the places were cool, temperature-wise because of the adobe. But a lot of the poorer people lived in tiny cubicles made from bamboo and lived with only a sheet for a wall. Any GI that ignored the huge signs we posted at the entrances immediately became a potential murder victim. They didn't all die surprised, some left signs of having struggled quite a bit. I don't know what would make a young GI risk his life to go into those places. The alleys were so narrow you couldn't pass another person without having to turn your shoulder. Maybe it was a thrill to go in there since everyday soldiering in Saigon could get pretty boring. Maybe the victims underestimated the danger, that's why they ignored the signs.

"The opportunities to screw up were always there, even in Saigon. Maybe especially in Saigon. The drive out to the rifle range was an example. It was a routine drive, so routine in fact that the VC were bound to figure it out and take full advantage of it. I remember saying, 'Somebody ought to change the schedule,' but nobody was listening. It didn't seem to matter. One day one of the other groups was out practicing their marksmanship and they were coming back carrying some ammo and stepped on a claymore. The other MPs ran over a hill and saw three Vietnamese in a rice paddy, running away. They killed them all with automatic weapons.

"It was sad because that entire incident could have been avoided and those lives could have been saved. As an MP, you were there to try to save lives, so it really hurt you to see that sort of thing.

"In '67 during a big Vietnamese celebration, the parade route wound near the MACV (Military Assistance Command Vietnam) compound where most of the generals stayed and which at that time was situated downtown. One of the duties of the MPs was to protect these generals, to provide escort for them. These MPs had the short-barreled M-16s with them and used a banana clip. They wore the soft baseball hat and some even wore civilian clothes. Well, at this celebration, the VC cut holes in the roofs of several houses in an adjacent residential area. From there they lobbed mortar rounds into the MACV compound. They also hit the parade, killing a lot of bystanders and hit some of the houses of the ARVN. Of course, the helicopter gunships were brought in and it got pretty hairy. During the fighting there was this reporter who wouldn't move out of the way even after he had been warned several times. Finally, this great big sergeant upended him with the stock of his grease gun. I think he bloodied him up, but that was the only way he was going to move. Then they picked up his camera and escorted him to the back."

Haight Ashbury

"If you think Saigon was a bizarre place, well maybe in some ways it was. Like the six bars that were off limits to whites. These bars were frequented by Blacks and were situated on the Saigon docks. But you know, usually there was never any trouble there, although a lot of the MPs were afraid to go there. Maybe not afraid, but they were uptight about it. But I was only hassled once while I was there. We always traveled in two's, but that was the same anywhere we went.

"I survived Saigon and flew back to the states and went to San Francisco, 'cause I had a brother that lived there. He worked in a restaurant. He took me to Haight Ashbury to show me the hippies. 'What in the hell is this?' I remember thinking.

"There were thousands of them, thousands of long-haired hippies at Haight Ashbury and there I was with my Army haircut and suit and hallucinating from the lack of sleep. All I wanted to do was get away from there and go sleep for three days. I couldn't seem to get enough sleep. I just wanted to sleep."

The Chill After Saigon

"When I was discharged from the service, I went to school in Everett at the Community College. I dropped out of there and wanted to become a police officer. I had enjoyed it when I was doing it in Saigon.

"I had looked at it and decided that was the type of job I wanted to do. So I applied for jobs at Sunnyside and Grandview.

(These are towns in the Lower Yakima Valley in South-Central Washington State.) The Chief of Police in Sunnyside was real cold, like he was looking down on me. The impression I received from the Chief in Sunnyside back then (circa 1967-68) was, 'What are you doing here, wetback?'

"I told him my qualifications. I felt I was qualified to take whatever training they might have. But he didn't even give me the opportunity to take the test. I know I didn't go in there with a chip on my shoulder; in fact, my wife was with me when I went in there. I was sincere.

"The Chief asked me if I was willing to arrest people that I had grown up with. I told him, 'If they're out of line, yes. That would be my duty.'

"His response was he didn't believe I could. The response was basically the same in Grandview. I never did move back to the Valley after the service. I had been living in Seattle and had gone to Sunnyside to apply at the Police Department. I just went back to Seattle."

Chapter Ten

Farewells Would Be Difficult

Antonio (Tony) Santoy

1969-70
U.S. Air Force

"All the military branches had men around the Da Nang area. How did they know where and how to meet? I guess it was the network. The word got out that Chicanos would meet in such and such an area . . . and people from all the branches would show up." Tony Santoy

Big Dinners
Monkey Mountain and Blueprints
Chicanos

Big Dinners

"The training in the Air Force was easy. The weather was another thing, but I got used to it. First, I was at Lackland in Texas, then I went to Biloxi, Mississippi for electronics training. They gave us the basic electronics course, then they broke us up into individual specialties like ground radio, airborne radio, radar, etc. I got 40 weeks of this stuff, then they put me in a two-week experimental course in digital techniques.

"There had been rumors that the Air Force didn't send you to Vietnam once you had been through a technical school that lasted 40 weeks, but I got my orders to go to Vietnam. They told me I was going to leave from McCord, so I told my parents, and of course, there was a big family reunion. There were *comidas por donde quiera* (several big dinners, a lot of getting together). I have family in all the little towns around here.

"Leaving Mom was hard, otherwise it wasn't too emotional. I was the only one still left in the family. Knowing that the farewells would be difficult to deal with, I had my sister take me to the airport so my folks wouldn't have to deal with it. The folks saw me the last time at the house. It was a seventeen hour flight from McCord to Anchorage then to Japan, and finally to Cam Rahn Bay.

"At Anchorage we ran into all these Army Airborne *locos* buying all these survival books and stuff on booby traps. Everybody headed to the bar as soon as we got to the airport. I think I downed four drinks in half-an-hour or an hour. Then we boarded a flight to Tachikawa, Japan and from there took a four-hour flight to Cam Rahn. We got there at midnight. I didn't know what to do or how to get to my squadron. I asked around and was told to call this number. The CQ (Charge of Quarters), a runner, came out to pick me up.

"Before landing at Cam Rahn Bay, they had warned us of a possible attack. There were two lights on as the plane circled. Everybody kept getting more and more paranoid as the plane kept circling. Instructions were to get to a bunker on the left. We were to run there and stay there. With all this going on, you felt helpless, like a sitting duck.

"The CQ picked me up and took me to squadron headquarters. He was driving without lights. That was to keep from attracting a sniper and also, the reflection from the moon probably provided enough light. The moon shone nicely on the water. We swung away around the beach and then to the barracks and company. The clerks there outfitted me with a rifle, a vest, helmet, canteen, *todo el pedo* (everything I needed), chow kit, etc.

Monkey Mountain and Blueprints

"At Cam Rahn I experienced a loss of direction, a real dislocation of feeling. There was no work for me to do at Cam Rahn Bay, no sense of purpose. My first two weeks in Vietnam were spent counting the minutes go by; I had no duties. I had been told during orientation that even though I was only an E-2, I would not pull any KP (Kitchen Patrol, i.e., dishwasher), no guard duty, or anything like that. My duty would be to install and maintain ground/air communication equipment and nothing else. At that point when I heard that that was what I would be doing, it made me feel worthwhile, like I could hold my head up high.

"I got a temporary duty assignment in a squadron that had people from all of the diverse fields of electronics. We also had some supply people. They then broke us up into groups of five or six, and a technical staff sergeant gave us our instructions.

"Behind our quarters they had the bunkers where you were supposed to go if you got shelled. These bunkers were rebuilt every three months because they tended to fall apart; the sacks would sag and rip and the sand would pour out. A lot of the guys used to hide their pot and money in the sandbags that made up the walls of the bunker.

"Most of the time the guys in the group would be out on assignment doing their work. There wasn't a lot of harassment. I didn't get harassed by the Lifers. We had only one supply sergeant or clerk who always stuck around the area. The rest of us were always in and out on assignment.

"The way it worked is that they would give us the blueprints and materials, give us a jeep or pickup and let us go. We had to install the equipment and also to check it out for quality control before turning it over to the local units. We did it for the Marines, the Army, and for civilians in addition to the Air Force.

"If we drew an assignment where there weren't any military facilities, that meant we drew extra pay for quarters.

"I did a job at Monkey Mountain, north of Da Nang. I flew there. Because of the nature of our work, we got priority on flights and ended up bumping Army and Air Force staff sergeants. During my tour in Vietnam, I flew around the country a lot. I had a lot of flexibility in my job and didn't have to deal with the regular military bullshit. At the time I hadn't thought it through, obviously, to see what all this was about. The norms and values in 'Nam were different from what we had experienced in the states. For example, at Monkey Mountain I could get off base by getting on an ambulance. The guy in charge was a 1st lieutenant who had been busted from a captain's rank . . . I don't know why. He did it as a favor for us. He dealt drugs and I suppose he used the ambulance as a vehicle for doing that type of work.

"When we completed our assignment on Money Mountain, the master sergeant, we called them *zebras* 'cause they had so many stripes on their sleeves, gave us fifteen bucks. 'Here's your fini party,' he said.

"I got drunk and got into trouble. There were eleven of us and about ten or eleven Marines and we went at it. The Master at Arms broke us up. It was an Air Force club but the Navy, Marines, and Army all used it. It was an NCO (Non-commissioned Officer) club but it was open to all.

"At Phu Bai there were no military quarters for us so we lived in a small town. We had to be off the street by 10pm so we held up in a hotel. It was a good deal since we got nine dollars a day per diem -- although we could wheel and deal to live on three dollars. What you did with the rest of the per diem) was your business, you could live with a local gal at no extra cost or you could go in with four or five other guys and split the rent in a hotel room. If you went with the girl, it only cost you ... maybe ... some extra pop or booze. Minor expenses.

Chicanos

"First time I came across a group of Chicanos there were all the services represented there. All the military branches that had men around the Da Nang area. How did they know where and how to meet? I guess it was the network. The word got out that Chicanos would meet in such and such an area and people from all the branches would show up. We'd get together, thirty or forty Chicanos from all the services and all ranks, except for commissioned officers.

"It was word of mouth.

"One guy was designated as the leader. He was a staff sergeant of average height, a light-compexioned Chicano from Texas. Edinburg, I believe.

"One guy had a reel-to-reel tape player. Another guy could cook. Guys that were cooks would sneak off flour, steaks, frijoles, and all of us would bring our own bottles. It was usually on a Sunday.

"We called it *'nuestra casa'*, etc. You were invited to cook what you knew how to cook.

"We had ice in styrofoam cases. If you know anything about the heat there, you know what I'm talking about.

"The technical sergeant and this master sergeant would be rolling tortillas and everybody would be getting down, really having a good time.

"Guys from Texas would be loaded to the gills. There were *friegos* (lots) from Texas and California. Lots of dudes from there.

"Couple of occasions those *vatos* (guys) de *Tejas* would go out and look for a fight. If they couldn't find one, they'd fight among themselves. Twenty minutes later they would embrace, and become real *camaradas* again, real emotional.

"This guy called Paladin would get loaded and try to sell a .38 pistol. He'd take the gun apart and show it to you to try to sell it. Paladin was a Marine.

"Another dude, un *mensito* (not bright), was called *El Caballo*, the Horse. He was a tall, lanky dude, *moreno*, not light-complexioned. He got so drunk he'd be standing there with a bottle in his hand like a zombie. Dude was really into knocking knuckles.

"Guys would walk up to him. '*Verdad, Caballo*. Ain't that the truth?'

"He would nod.

" '*Verdad Caballo. Deme cinco*, give me five.' They would go through the routine, exchanging greetings by knocking knuckles. It was a Vietnam ritual.

"There were a lot of *chingazos*, fights, but not along the lines of Texas against California.

"No women to be had over there so we got together and got wasted."

Chapter Eleven

Going to the Fish Market

Antonio (Tony) Santoy

U.S. Air Force, Enlisted
1969-70

"Most of the time we were speaking Spanish to each other. You want to know if my team members complained or made any comments while I was talking to these guys? I didn't pay any attention to it." Tony Santoy

Green In-Country
The Good Technician
Identity: Shake The Skin Loose
The Chicano Get-Togethers

Green In-Country

You ask if I traveled a lot while I was in Vietnam. Yes, I did. For starters, I was assigned to an installation squadron in Cam Rahn Bay. That's where our headquarters was. It was to the North of Saigon right along the coast. It was an R&R (Rest & Recuperation) site. It was rather nice. Nothing but sand, and beach.

(Pause)

Well, it reminded me of a labor camp. We had these little hootches with tin roofs. It was just a shell actually, just the outside walls. There were six guys assigned to each hootch. In our hootch we added a section to the back and put up some screens so we had a little patio.

These were all Air Force guys. Yeah, it was an Air Force squadron. It was an installation squadron that would install electronic equipment. We were based right there at Cam Rahn Bay, that's where our supplies and personnel office were headquartered. Our central headquarters was there. The function of an installation squadron, which we called a GS squadron, was to set up electronic equipment. We were broken down into groups by specialty, by MOS (Military Occupation Specialty), if you will.

When I arrived I was assigned to a team. Initially, there were four of us. Orders would be cut for a team to go and set up some equipment. Within each team a senior ranking individual would be designated as the person in charge. We would fly in, we would secure transportation, our equipment would be flown in, we would pick it up, we'd take it on site -- we had to already know where the schematics were -- there would be schematics already available. So we would work just from schematics to set up the ground radio equipment.

Yeah, you've got the right impression that in the Air Force we didn't have to put up with a lot of bullshit like in the Army. That was the case with me.

You've also got it right that we were almost like civilians. That was really the case with me. It was. It was exactly like that. I always thought I had lucked out because of my MOS. And the fact that I was temporary duty. You know I had a home base but most of my work took me away from my assigned base.

I guess I was at Cam Ranh about a week and a half and I got my first assignment. It was to fly in with the whole team, there were four of us -- to a site . . .

Yes, at the airbase, we did run into other people who had the freedom to move around. They seemed to move around the country real easy. These were Warrant Officers and some other specialists. We worked with a couple of guys -- especially at Monkey Mountain -- who were Crypto specialists. They'd go in and overhaul the little gizmos in the back of the radios or wherever they were located. That's basically all they did.

Yeah, these were enlisted men, but they had a specialty all of their own. Top secret clearance and all of that stuff. Nobody was allowed in the area where they were, whereas ours was generally more open.

When I got to Long Binh, I was green. I didn't go downtown or anything. We were just there for two days, so I just stayed in the barracks, and didn't even go to the enlisted men's club. I just stayed in your hootch. Some of the other guys who had been there longer took off, but I don't know where they went. I just stayed close.

There I had my first experience with rats. I saw this great big ol' rat in one of the larger hootches. It was walking along the frame on a two-by-four. A fat one. A big juicy son-of-a-gun. I thought it was a cat, man. That thing was big! It didn't seem to bother anything or anybody.

Co-existence. Yeah. I wanted to talk about one more thing before I moved on. At Long Binh was where I first heard the mortars going off. It was like the Fourth of July. Everything was calm and it was hot -- not extremely hot, but humid -- during the day. We got back from working and everything was going like normal; it was like a regular job. You'd get up in the morning, eat breakfast and go do our installation work. We'd go home in the evening. Then about one in the morning, or maybe two or two-thirty we heard this fireworks going off. It was just a couple of loud noises and we could feel shaking a little bit and that was it. We didn't really have enough time to wake up that first time to get worried about what was going on before it was over.

Once we would fly in, pickup the equipment and install it, have it checked out, and turn it over, our job was done.

No, I didn't hear a lot of stories of the Tet Offensive of 1968. Not that many stories but bits and pieces while looking through the fences -- or especially in the Saigon area. I'd often wonder why they had broken glass cemented on top of these fences and it was just a normal occurrence, the way things were done.

A lot of the buildings were dilapidated and the back sections were torn out or patched up. Certain areas within the city -- just like any large city, I guess -- were covered with potholes, muddy, and infested with flies.

Lots of refugees. Yeah, a transient population.

War refugees from the countryside poured into the city. In some parts of the city huge piles of trash-- as big as a house -- stood in the middle of the road. Because of the war, and perhaps corruption in the South Vietnamese government, there was no waste removal.

We did a small job on Ton Son Nhut on the outskirts of Saigon. I think it was our second job. As I recall, it was to the west of Saigon. Anyway, I remember driving out and seeing this old tank ditched along the side of the road. You have to understand we didn't have much time to look around because the transmitter and receiver sites were mostly located on opposite sides of the control towers which meant that you either had to go around or through the runways. If you drove across the runways you had to get clearance from the tower. And if you drove around it, it was usually the perimeter. It wasn't advisable to be stopping and checking things out because the Military Police would stop by to see what you were doing.

Anyway, we took a couple of days and finally decided to stop and check what this large contraption was. It was like an antiquated tank, is what it was. It was a French tank. Something had gone wrong with it and it had just been abandoned there. We checked it out. It looked antique.

We were always in teams on Monkey Mountain. We would travel as a team, we would work outside as a team, and when we came back we hung around together so the structure kind of encouraged that.

You'll recall I arrived in-country by myself. I had basically two immediate circles that I dealt with. One was at my home base where I had these five or six guys that were in the same hootch. They were in supply and were installing antennas and were in a variety of MOS's. But still we had one thing in common, which was the area in which we slept. The other was the team.

The Good Technician

The team would be put together for a certain project. See when I left tech school and went over to Vietnam, my MOS still required further study and a test before to be eligible for the next grade. It was something like an apprenticeship. So when I got into country we had a lot of problems setting up a program for me, a correspondence program so that I would get the materials, and arrange for a training officer. The trainer assigned to me was a guy from California. A very competent individual, he had served as a forward observer in support of ground forces. He had a lot of technical experience; he was a very good technician, excellent. He was my trainer and I didn't have any problems in training in the functional aspects of my MOS.

I learned quickly to do what I needed to do. I became fairly competent. But the other part of my training fell out and it took us about six months to get the correspondence course.

I learned quickly because we worked as a team. It was like OJT (on-the-job training). My training officer was a staff sergeant. I had a basic knowledge, but he taught us the wiring and how to read the schematics. We had just gotten a basic course in schematic reading. I knew how to read schematics internally, in a radio, but I did not have the knowledge to read the schematics of a building and how you set up the equipment, the layout.

Our schematics were perhaps six or eight large schematics that showed you different views of different things. One would give you the entire layout of a building and where the radios were set up. Another schematic would have the wiring, the electrical power source. Another was for the antennas, another for the audio wires, another for the other systems that were to be installed: for example, the resonators, the relays, the tape recorders, those kinds of things. He led me through that whole process. As I said, he was an extremely sharp individual, competent. Very easy going.

Let me put this into perspective. I didn't have the pressures as a new individual in the unit simply because of my relationships within my circles.

Tony Santoy (center) with unidentified fellow airmen in Vietnam.

When I was at Monkey Mountain we went to Saigon for about three weeks after Long Binh. Saigon was a large city. We landed in Ton Son Nhut. It was all Air Force.

We worked right *on* the airbase. I was still fairly new then but I began to notice the difference between various sites. Tan Son Nhut was a much larger airbase and was located on the outskirts of a large city. Because of the large Air Force component there, there was a lot more structure. It was more rigid in that we were expected to salute and to comply with all of those regs. As far as a working environment it was not very conducive in that you had to worry about the bullshit. You had to worry about getting from one place to another, hoping like hell you didn't meet an officer and have to salute. You were always taking a chance you'd get chewed out for somethin' or other. You had to watch your P's and Q's all the time.

While in Saigon I think we installed a couple of radios. Oh, yeah, we got into the city. Now that was a mind-blower! I went down to Plantation Road. Yeah, I heard that snipers killed both Vietnamese and Americans along Plantation Road during the Tet Offensive. But all I saw when I was there were prostitutes! Still, there was a Chinese restaurant I always used to go to. I got to know some of the people that worked there.

I heard about people getting sick from eating in the local restaurants, but I think that was from a nervous condition. I really don't think it was the water . . . because on most bases it was heavily chlorinated. In the city it wasn't. Well, I never really worried about that. I didn't worry about the food. The food didn't seem to bother me. I worried more about the water.

I would always go down to a Chinese restaurant. The food was good. The Ngoc Mum, I didn't like. Ngoc Mum was a kind of an oil-base spice. Ah, man, it was strong. Not even mosquitoes would come around. Really potent. But, you know, the rice and meat, the gravy and ... It was like Chinese food but a little more bland, but it was good.

Not everybody would eat there. Some of the guys were really finicky and wouldn't have it.

GI's varied in how they would venture out into the city. In Saigon, some would go to work, and back, and they never ventured into the city. If they did, it would be in large groups where they would feel secure, some carrying their cameras to record their adventure for posterity. Others went to the other extreme, basically going native among the Saigonese, when not on duty.

It was a heavy time. When I went to Saigon -- I think it must have been the first or second time. I had met this guy that was from California. He was installing antennas and he was really a dope fiend. This guy would go downtown and buy these packs of cigarettes. It was a pack of weed instead of regular tobacco. And he'd always hide a few joints in his pack of regular cigarettes. So when he'd climb those poles -- these 20 and 30 foot poles -- to mount antennas and hook up the wires, he'd be up there all by himself. And he'd always be gettin' high! And he said he loved it.

He said he'd be seeing tech sergeants and staff sergeants and all kinds of people with rank down there watchin' him and here he'd be out there in plain sight just blowin' his brains away! He said nobody knew the difference.

Anyway, this guy invited me to downtown Saigon. It was really weird because I remember it was on a Sunday morning. We got out and I mean it was early. We decided to go to the fish market. So we got up, got dressed, headed off base and we climbed on one of these motorcycles that had the seat up front. Remember those?

These were motorized rickshaws.

Yeah, the others were called Lambrettas, the little trucks. Then there were the little French-made taxis, the little blue and white ones. I never rode in a taxi; but we used to *love* to ride cyclos. Anyway, so we climbed onto one of these. He said, "Listen, we're going to go down to the fish market. You'll really like this." I don't know whether he meant to do this or not but he was talking about where we were going and I was just trippin' on what was happenin'!

Yeah, because as soon as we got off base the guy lights up a joint and I wasn't used to this. This is the same guy that was up on the power pole toking up. So we walked for a little bit, we smoked this joint and I took a few puffs and I got into the happenin's there. I started experiencing this lightness, you know, a kind of happy, warm feeling inside. And then we climb out to this cyclo -- by this time this guy is really *out there.* He starts talkin' like Wolf Man Jack. He starts talkin' like Wolf Man Jack to the cyclo driver! You know, "Hey, come on baby" and all that kind of stuff. (Laughter) So we climbed in and he tells this guy where we're headed and this is a new experience for me, right? It's blowin' me away, right? Nothing in front of you, you're just tooteling down the street, buildings going all over the place. It's early in the mornin' . . .

We must have been doin' 30, 40, 50 miles an hour, and it's like riding on a car bumper! Nobody on the streets 'cause it's six or seven in the morning. Oh, yeah! If there was any traffic, you gotta be figuring out how you're going to keep from getting your toes smashed!

That was typical. But they were just daredevil drivers. Imagine that kind of experience and then being high. And then to hear this guy talkin' just like Wolf Man Jack. "Have mercy, baby. Give 'er hell!" and all this bullshit. It's six o'clock in the morning and we're going fifty miles an hour down the streets of Saigon.

So we went to the fish market. It was smelly, muddy, and . . . and not a lot of people there walking around. Not initially. Eventually there were. But we were mostly there in the morning. They had crabs, a variety of fish at different stands. They had shaded areas. Just like a little carnival. It was mostly Vietnamese. Especially early in the morning.

Later in the day there might be an incredible heat, and it might get muggy. There was the heavy rain but also beautiful mornings --you had to be there all year to go through these different seasons. But there was a time of the year when the mornings would be cool, calm. A near paradise. In that serenity transcending the war, the Vietnamese moved gracefully in their light weight or silk clothes. That's what it was like. And it was a good time of the day to get from one place to another. You could really enjoy it, as you weren't caught in that trap with all the traffic.

Later on it just got incredible with all the noise, the heat, and the flies. But in the morning, as you weren't hurrying around, it was cool, it was silent, it was peaceful. You could do your thing, enjoy it, enjoy the scenery, or whatever you were doing, if you were traveling or if you were walking, and really focus on that.

There was the Continental Palace Hotel, not far from the expensive red-light district on Tu Do Street. The Congress Building was not far from the Continental Palace. Plantation Road, on the other hand, veered Southwest from the main airport, Tan Son Nhut.

I don't know if I ever told you that, but my thing was selling cognac. I'd sell cognac on the Black Market for a little profit to support my little ventures. A couple of guys on the team or some friends of theirs would buy some bottles for me at the PX (Post

Exchange) with their liquor rations. I'd put them all in a big travel bag, as many bottles as I could get, anywhere from 8 to 13, and occasionally I'd go down to Saigon and sell 'em on the Black Market.

The cost at the PX was $2.75 or $3.75, something like that.

I'd sell them to the Vietnamese for eleven to thirteen dollars. I didn't worry about getting caught because it was so common. Mine was petty stuff. There were a lot of people that were selling refrigerators, televisions.

The U.S. allies, the Koreans and Thais, would buy up all the refrigerators and air conditioners as soon as they were delivered at the PX. They'd back up a couple of trucks and load all refrigerators and air conditioners they could get and take them straight to the Black Market. It was rumored that the Thais would buy everything they could and ship it to Thailand.

The more I became acclimated and orientated to the happenings, to the rules of the game, I guess, the more chances I would take. So this helped to make life easier, a little bit of money. You could support your little ventures.

So that was my thing, my way of financing, selling cognac I knew a couple of shops right off Ton Son Nhut airbase where I could go to sell the cognac. The rest of the time I just caught a cyclo. I sold a fan once but that was the largest item I sold.

It was a wide open city where you could buy anything you wanted. I saw one guy, I don't know if he was a Navy gunner or something. He was Special Forces of some kind. Up on Monkey Mountain, this guy walked into the NCO Club and he had a little ball chain. He must've had ten, eleven ears. Souvenirs. This guy was a little crazy. He got a few drinks down his belly and started breaking glasses and acting out.

A lot of veterans had severe problems when they got back home. Much of the population had turned against the war, and many blamed the individual veterans personally.

When we got home there was the fear . . . I think that family members or friends or other individuals may want to learn about your perspective but they may not necessarily approve of it. Do you understand what I'm saying? There's a curiosity. But they may not necessarily approve of your role or your behavior or your thoughts.

From my perspective, though it was reassuring in one sense. If you understand that I was going through a very confusing chapter in my life, from a cultural standpoint it was positive.

It served to confirm some of my inner beliefs. About myself and my status. The status of *my* family, as compared to the "standard, typical American family." Do you understand what I'm saying in that the standard environment was perpetuated and reinforced in American society. And the value system, the economic status, the definition of the "thing to do." It was different for my family unit and for me.

And I always felt that I should hide this or I want to conceal it. I didn't have quite the same value system, the same upbringing, the same standards.

Identity: Shake the Skin Loose

When I went into the Air Force, then to Vietnam, I was exposed to people not only from the Yakima Valley, but from all over Washington, and not only from all over Washington, but from New York City, Louisiana and California. It was enough to shake the skin loose, so to speak.

I dealt with people away from their ties, away from that pressure to maintain the status quo, the moral standards, the ethical standards, the sterile environment, that whole conservative structure, part of that. I think it was being rebelled against here in the states. That whole redefinition of equal rights, civil liberties, this anti-discrimination, that kind of thing.

Of course, that was a phase that the country went through as a whole. But over there you were able to see it on a more personal basis, to see it on a larger scale. It wasn't just individuals lumped together. It wasn't just the younger generation that were rabble-rousers. It was noticing that whole difference: how people lived, how people made a living, how people saved their money, what they cherished. What their priorities were and how they aligned their priorities; how they placed values on different things.

My perceptions while growing up were that you felt that you were in a somewhat sterile environment brought on by the society that's in control here. By the standards set here. By the standard, conservative environment -- and going into the Army, and living in Vietnam, all this sort of thing, probably even in training, I were exposed to a much broader range of opinions about things.

That, plus seeing the life-style of the Vietnamese which was also different. Being over there served as a positive reinforcement so that I began to look at my place not only within a state or a nation but just as a human being, and it all of a sudden it dawned on me -- for example, the fact that I was Hispanic, that I was Chicano, that my roots were back in Mexico, that some parts of Mexico were very poor, that we like *nopales* (prickly pear cactus, for eating), that we did some farming -- and that that was not all wrong. They ate fresh fruit there in Vietnam. There were different types of fruit, different types of dishes.

They saved money in a different way; they bought jewelry and made their investments -- maybe not everybody, but at least some of the classes in that society would save money in that way.

It was probably the safe way in an unstable society given the state of the nation and the economy. There was a struggle to survive.

There was a reassurance that if you step beyond the individual, beyond the family, beyond the community, beyond the state, beyond the nation that we, as Chicanos, having a Mexican background and those kinds of roots were different from the standard "clean cut American", and that that encompassed a majority of this world. It wasn't the reverse, as I had believed. I was *not* the minority. On an international basis, I was part of the majority. That was okay.

In terms of learning the game of life -- for me -- it represented that whole notion of blending but setting the limits and being selective. And really recognizing those differences and learning how to deal with those differences.

I'm not sure how much having been a member of a two-child family and being a loner contributed to that. The other element was the fact that with my Air Force specialty I wasn't bogged down with military duties. I didn't have guard duty, kitchen duty, or . . . I had some freedom to explore. I had flexibility. I felt that I didn't have as big of blinders on.

I became a regular at a couple of restaurants. I'd eat breakfast at the airbase when I was there but whenever I'd go downtown, I'd make it a point to stop. I loved rice. Fried rice.

So then I had my three weeks in Saigon, or three months, whatever. I was pulled back into Cam Rahn Bay and reassigned along with ten other guys and then we went up to Monkey Mountain. Now, Monkey Mountain is where I used to get together with the Chicanos on Sundays down at the base. There was a little compound at the base of the mountain. But I mean at the Da Nang airbase, which was down closer to the shore. So we went to Monkey Mountain, and lived in that little compound for five months.

What we did was called a "rehab." We tore out everything and reinstalled every piece of equipment. It was over 100, closer to 130 or 150 radio receivers. It was all in one large building.

There was not a heavy guard around the area, just concertina wire. I suppose the VC could have easily gone in there and blown up the equipment, but they didn't. It was patrolled but it wasn't posted with guards.

The equipment at Monkey Mountain was resonators. They were a piece of equipment, cube-shaped, that allowed you to plug in -- it had tanks inside . . . I never got into the guts of it. But it was a piece of equipment that enabled you to plug in perhaps four radios and put them on one antenna so that you wouldn't tie up one antenna for one radio.

So you can plug in maybe a total of four or eight radios on one antenna. The antenna would pick up all these different frequencies and break them out by frequency so that you could hook up. You could operate four or eight transmitters or receivers on one antenna.

The "zebra," the sergeant with all the stripes was in charge of the team. He would just be overseeing. He was an alright guy, a very devout, military person. He was a technician of sorts, a specialist. He knew, or at least gave the appearance of understanding the overall process. He was the one who carried around the schematics and he was the one that oversaw the whole operation.

We lived in that compound at the base of the mountain. And every morning we would get up and have breakfast at a messhall. Then we'd drive on up to the hill. Take a jeep up a winding road. There were no operators inside that building; it was just a physical location. We weren't privy to exactly how it worked, but part of it was tapped in to Da Nang airbase. I don't know where the rest of it was hooked up to because there was a *lot* of equipment. It was a ground-to-air traffic communications site: it was called a "gator".

Monkey Mountain was a wooded area of broadleaf trees and brush. There used to be rock apes there. The whole time -- I don't know what happened to them -- but . . . I know I only saw a couple of rock apes ...

Note: This part of the discussion ended with a brief conversation about the fate of the rock apes. As there were many compassionate soldiers in Vietnam, there were also soldiers who too easily used their weapons. This part of the conversation ended without a resolution.

The Chicano Get-Togethers

We got together maybe four or five times the year I was there. We got together at Da Nang. It was interesting how the network was developed. We had guys that were with the Marines, Navy folks, we had Air Force, we had Army, and the word would get out about when we were going to meet. That was important because where I was at there were no Blacks, no other Chicanos.

I think on a Sunday we went down to the NCO club or one of the clubs down in Da Nang. And that was one of the meeting places. So I ran into some Chicanos down there. I was with my buddies on the team, right? We walked in and there were some of them standing there or you said "hey, man" or "what's going on?" We were all there drinking at separate tables and then the Chicanos just came by. Then I got introduced to a couple of people. As a matter of fact, one of the cooks in Da Nang was from my home town.

Most of the time we were speaking Spanish to each other.

You want to know if my team members complained or made any comments while I was talking to these guys? I didn't pay any attention to it. The Chicanos invited me down for the get-together, so on a Sunday I got a ride from one of the Navy guys. He came by the compound and picked me up.

You know, it was interesting that I met this cook there who used to run around with one of my cousins in Edinburg, Texas. I was four or five when my dad moved the family from Edinburg to the Yakima Valley. (Pause) Anyway, it was really interesting that he . . . I can't remember how we found out that he happened to know my brother, or I mean my cousin.

We had some good friendships. There at the compound there was also a pastry cook who was from Corpus Christi, Texas. I got to know him really well. He was Chicano. I lost track of him. After the war I ran into him at McConnel Air Force base in Kansas. (Reflecting back) Arnold Torres. Good pastry man. He would make terrific doughnuts and pies.

I got along well with Chicanos from Texas, but some Californians did not always get along with the guys from Texas. There was a little bit of mismatch there. Because the guys from California were much more aggressive, outgoing and seemed much more assimilated.

The guys from Texas held strong to their values, their likes and dislikes and were more Chicano oriented; you know, more of a separate society type of relationship.

As a matter of fact, two of my friends, one was from California and that guy from Texas, got into it. There was a mismatch in how they saw things and how they thought. They got into a big fight but this happened back in the states.

Anyway, Arnold, who was from Corpus, I later ran into -- that's what I wanted to focus on. So I got some more pastries from him! Just like old times! In the states, hell, I'd get whole pies and cookies and doughnuts and all that kind of stuff that he would make. He'd always send me a plate of something. (Long pause) Anyway, it blew me away, to find that there was a group of Chicanos that would come together and play Mexican music and make their own food and have their own get-togethers. It served its purpose and it was well-organized for the purpose it had. It was a place where you could establish some friendships and a vehicle by which you could partake in an activity that you could feel comfortable in. In some ways it was a suitable substitute for the activities that used to take place at home.

The fact that the guys would steal steak, and steal *arroz* (rice) and *frijoles* (beans) and make tortillas and somebody would bring in a reel-to-reel tape recorder with a bunch of contemporary Chicano music: Little Joe, Tortilla Factory, and Sonora Santanera; all those different types, Augustin Ramirez and all that type of music which was really going heavy, selling hot and heavy over there. I still go to dances once in a while. I do it once or twice a year.

Note: Military literature is replete with units "appropriating" (stealing) supplies from other units, etc. Officially it's frowned upon, but unofficially it's winked at, as long as it is to be used within the military.

Chapter Twelve

A Full Circle

A Marine in Vietnam

Lionel Guerra
U.S. Marine Corps
1967-68

". . . and it was here that we started hearing Vietnam stories from veterans. These stories made you want to go out and kill, but you never think they will kill you." Lionel Guerra

A Tale of the Iron Fist: Marine Basic
Map Reading and Live Rounds
The Knots We Learned to Tie
Like Discovering Dinosaurs
In a Field of Elephant Grass
Hill 881 North

A Tale of the Iron Fist: Marine Basic

"I graduated from high school in June, 1966, and went into the Marines in August. I had asked my parents about going in and they had been kind of hesitant. The Marines finally got me when I got caught drinking after football season. I had drunk only half bottle of beer, but the problem was that the guys who purchased the beer were seventeen years old and I was eighteen. We also had some girls with us, and their father had been following us. I remember the girls yelling 'don't stop' when they saw him -- but crazy me -- I saw a red light and stopped and their father curved in front of us with his car.

"The police were called and I spent one day in jail and got fined two-hundred thirty dollars. Being the oldest one in the family, and having just graduated from high school, it was disgraceful for me to be bailed out of jail by my parents. I had been All-Valley left guard and had gotten the 'most inspirational' award for my team, but now I had disappointed my parents. I didn't want to get married, and I had no money, so I called the recruiting station in Yakima and asked about the Marines. They said I could go for six years, or five, four or three. I went in for three.

"I signed the papers to join the Marine Corps at the Granger Post Office. (Editor: Granger is a small farming community in South Central Washington state.) Anyway, they gave me a ticket to Seattle, and I took the preliminary tests, and flew to San Diego. When we got there this one guy in charge at the Depot came out and said to us, 'You maggots wait outside and don't move from where you are.'

"Then the van came to pick us up. I was smiling and talking and this guy came up and yelled 'Shut up.' Right in my face, and I thought 'Hey man, these guys mean business.'

"At the Marine Corps barracks they had us line up and everything was traumatic. We had our heads shaved. Suddenly all my hair was gone and I was in a daze because I didn't feel the same. We all walked around looking at each other. A lot of things surprised me, and I didn't know about any of this that they were going to do. I was green. I didn't know how to make a bed and I hardly knew anything about a rifle. I didn't know the parts of a rifle. I had shot my friend's rifles but that was all, just a few times.

"One time we were in our dungarees and the sergeant said, 'Everybody should have x number of magazines' and I thought 'Oh, boy, we get to read!' I couldn't find the magazines I was supposed to have in my equipment.

"Another time I got my finger caught in the bolt and man, that hurt. I remember the first night one guy showed me how to make my bed and I slept on top. I didn't want to mess it up by crawling in the sheets. After a few days I got the courage to go under but I didn't move.

"I weighed 172 and told myself I was going to lose some weight. I was strong; when I worked for Del Monte Corporation I had asked for the job pulling reborts that weighed 1500 pounds. They had said I was 'too small' to do the job, but I had told them I could do it.

"The first time we went to chow I decided I wasn't going to eat breakfast because I was going to get into shape. I wanted to lose weight and go for a PT record so I told the Drill Instructor I wasn't going to eat breakfast. Well, the workout that morning was so bad that I could hardly drag myself around, and I told myself, 'Never will I miss breakfast again.'

"One time we were lined up outside cleaning our rifles and I couldn't put my firing spring back together. The Filipino Gunnery Sergeant came over. 'What's the matter, boy?'

"'Sir, I can't put my firing pin back.'

"He looks at it and hits my left shoulder with the butt of the rifle.

"I made a slow fist and wanted so bad to hit him.

"He stared at me and I looked back.

"'What's the matter boy, how come you keep on eyeball fuckin' me?' he finally said. He fixed the rifle and left.

"Another time this Drill Instructor said, 'You an Indian boy?'

"I said, 'No, Mexican, sir.'

"He looked at me, maybe because of my nose and black hair and said, 'You look like an Indian to me.'

"Back at the barracks I just about got into a fight with my bunkmate. It was just hard to get used to the system. We had this one drill instructor who was a playboy type, a real sadistic person. He would force us to exercise, exercise, exercise in the sun. He had us doing pullups on our elbows. He would scream at us.

"I was in line taking the PT test and this Chicano told me, 'That *bolillo* over there in that platoon has his shit together.' (Editor: Pronounced bo lee' oh, *bolillos* are white balls of dough, the way Mexicans often think of Anglo Saxons. It can be an innocuous term.) Anyway, this *bolillo* was really doing well in the PT test. I wanted to do well because I took a lot of pride in being able to perform. I fixed my gaze on that guy and began to meditate on beating him. He did 20 military pullups where you have to pull yourself overhead each time. I concentrated and did that many too. Next he did 60 pushups and I did sixty pushups. That was no problem because I like pushups. Then we had to do 41 squat thrusts in two minutes. I only did 37. Then we had to do about 60 situps in two minutes. It was like that, nip and tuck, the whole way, with him doing something and me trying to outdo him.

"Finally we got to the 440 yard run and I thought, 'Good, I got ya.'

"The 440 yard run is a hard run, once around the track in combat boots. But I used to run the 440 in the mile relay in high school. It was a coincidence that I got the *bolillo* with me in the same race. I won but I was exhausted when it was over. It's not like in high school where you're fresh for a race and don't wear combat boots.

"Later on this DI walked in at chow and hollered, 'Which ones Guerra?' All the shave-head trainees turned around to see who it was. 'See that boy there, he scored the highest in the three battalions,' he said. I had scored 487 points out of a possible 500 points. That was the breakthrough for me. My responsibilities from then on were to train the fat boys. I didn't have to train anymore or pull KP. I just trained the fat boys in the fat platoon. I trained them in the morning. But I continued to work hard because that is what had gotten me this break. I used to stay up at night after lights out and do pushups. I wanted to do well.

"There were a lot of odd things that happened and they stay fresh in your mind because there were few distractions. This Black guy tried to get out of the Marines as a queer, but later I saw him in another platoon so he must have been recycled.

"They taught us how to swim the hard way. We just got thrown in. First they made us jump wearing shorts and then we were told to wear our boots. I jumped but I remember one guy, another Mexican, didn't want to jump and the sergeant, who was also a Chicano, yelled, 'Get in there Mexican!' That memory just came back to me. It didn't seem right.

"There weren't very many Chicanos that were Platoon Sergeants, just staff and gunnery. There were a lot of politics that I didn't know about then. I just accepted things as they were until promotions came around and you began to see the politics.

"I knew a guy from Mexico who had the option to join the service. There were a lot of others. This guy got wounded and had his two legs amputated, but he came back as an American citizen. I don't remember if he was bitter, but he said he was going back to Mexico to retire.

"Time went by fast at times, slow at other times. I remember the mirror and practicing to salute. They told us the mirror didn't lie. So I would practice. Then I'd be thinking, thinking: 'What am I going to eat?' The exercise and drill would make you hungry. I thought about food as a way to rest; it was a mental rest as well.

"They began to teach us to work together. If we caught a guy from another platoon by himself we would break ranks and march around him but we would beat him up. We would take side steps but stay in ranks. This was the beginning of the training that teaches you to do everything together because otherwise everyone will suffer together.

"I remember the shock of being in the Marines. They had us lined up, lots of us, naked. And we counted off. When you'd walk up to the doctor somebody would yell 'Number 30, 30 cock' and you had to pull the skin back. They checked your teeth too, and your nails.

"The training continued. It was 'kill, kill, kill.' We wore padding and fought with each other. We saw films, sang songs, and learned the codes. We learned the Marine Corps song step-by-step. We'd finish lunch, then march from class to class, 'One, two, three, four, we are the best.' It went on and on. I remember looking at the planes overhead and thinking 'What am I doing here? When will I get out?' Mail call was depressing. They would throw your letters on the ground. If you got some cake, you would have to eat it all in front of the whole company. They would throw the letters at you and tell you to open them with your toes. They even told you when you could take a shit."

Map Reading and Live Rounds

"In ITR (Infantry Training Regiment) we got *pogey* babe (Editor's note: Marine slang for sweets or some other reward), got to go to the movies. We went to the movies in another base. They took us there by bus.

"We still did a lot of walking. I remember getting shin splints. It seemed like we were always marching, running, walking. I got shin splints all the time. We were always stretching so we could get into different firing positions. We learned to fire the M-60 machinegun and the M-79 grenade launcher. It's a short stubby little weapon. But they still threw our letters in the sand and made us crawl down to get them. I was in a different platoon now, with different people.

"Alvarado was a sergeant there and there were some other Chicanos. They taught us how to hold the arm and elbow in a sling for a steadier aim. We did a lot of stretching so we could shoot from a squatting or sitting position. We bivouacked for two days.

"During ITR we got to wear our complete uniforms for the first time, and on the weekends we could go to Hollywood. Four of us went to the Boulevard but there was too much trouble there. We got a motel room, and when we went back outside, I remember seeing this girl and whistling and saying, 'Look at that!' She was blond and was wearing tight jeans but it turned out that *she* was a guy. We just weren't used to the long hair and tight jeans back then.

"We were all Marines and didn't have relatives there so we pooled our money for a motel room. We just watched tv, ate, relaxed. One time we went to the grocery store and met this pro boxer, a Black guy. He invited us to his place and showed us around.

"Other weekends we went to L.A. We took the bus from the base north of San Diego (whereas Basic had been at Camp Pendleton).

"I knew how to make friends, but sometimes I was apprehensive because I had come to San Diego alone. In ITR they told us to call the trainer 'sergeant' rather than 'sir'. They went about teaching you that you were indestructible.

"In ITR we lived in quonset huts but now we moved into concrete quarters for AIT (Advanced Individual Training). The food got better and there was no more yelling. We had all received different orders. These were all Infantry people, all specialists. We got into map reading and maneuvered under live rounds. They taught us the U-and L-shaped ambushes.

"It was here that I first told the sergeant I wanted to be in Force Recon and was told that I had to have 20-20 eyesight.

"Here they were picky about our field gear and our basic dress. We went on more night maneuvers. They wanted to toughen you mentally, but there was still no talk of Vietnam-style booby traps.

"Before we were scheduled to go on leave a guy caught spinal meningitis and we were quarantined for two weeks. We had nothing to do but eat and read for the longest two weeks you could imagine.

"Whenever you go somewhere the Marines give you a two-way ticket. By this time they've taught you to respect other people by respecting yourself. When I got to go on leave, I was suddenly on my own and everything was different, exciting, and frightening. I had a ticket to LA., then to the airport. After the flight to Seattle, I had to wait all night for transportation and ended up sleeping in the airport.

"After leave I was supposed to go to the 1st Marine Division at Camp Lejune, North Carolina where I would be with the 1st Recon Battalion which is connected to the Infantry.

"We were stationed by the beach where we could practice capsizing a boat. We had to learn how to recover a boat or raft that had gotten flipped over. We also had to do 40 to 80 foot repelling off a tower. We learned rope tying, more map reading, and went on night patrols. They sent us out in squads to find certain points.

"One time this sergeant told me, 'Lionel, I want you to go out and find this tower.'

"So I took off. I went walking, walking, walking. Finally I couldn't find it and I thought I better get back. But I couldn't and I figured I was lost. I knew this Chicano named Carizales who was a corporal while I was only a private, so I went about in the woods *gritando* (yelling) 'Carizales!' I would yell then I would walk a little bit and then I would yell again, 'Carizales!' hoping somebody would hear me.

"They had the helicopters looking for me. In fact the whole company was looking for me. I was finally found by another squad of the same company, but when they found me their radio wouldn't work. There was no way they could call in to stop the search. After a while they had the whole battalion looking for me and had an alert out for the whole base.

"The sergeant couldn't believe it. 'Just go to bed,' he said.

"Carizales, the *Tejano* (Texan), just laughed. *Tejanos* swore a lot."

The Knots We Learned to Tie

"The training came in handy in Vietnam. The knots we learned to tie were used in repelling over there. In Vietnam, a Hawaiian named Kalama used such a knot to help us cross a river. He was about 6'2" and a good swimmer but he had to struggle hard against a strong current with a rope tied around his waist. Once he got across we used the rope like a pulley to pull our clothes and guns across.

"When I went to the 1st Recon we were stationed next to the ocean. It was beautiful, and we did a lot of running on the beach, both as part of our training and by ourselves. It was here that I finally met somebody in the service that was involved in the martial arts. I met this Vietnam veteran who was a second degree black belt and was teaching self-defense for ten dollars a month.

"In the military you do as much as you can to learn to protect yourself, and karate is just another part of it. It carries over to everyday life. Even now (1985), some mornings I don't even want to get up and I wonder why do I go on taking it. It's probably because of my military experience that I can go on. The Marine Corps trains you mentally so that when it comes down to the real thing you don't break down. They push, push, push you in basic so that you do break down. You are put under all this stress so that you can learn to throw a grenade and react to live bullets because in combat everything suddenly comes alive. Suddenly everything that in training was just a target is moving and shooting back at you. That is the big difference between training and Vietnam.

"In 1st Recon, we were back to spit shine boots, to a short haircut like in Basic. It was just as rough as Basic, and they treated you like you were back in Basic Training. After AIT, we were back to starched dungarees. We had a lot of cleanup details and a lot of classes and conditioning.

"We were given this little red book that showed how to use the choppers. We'd say 'Bravo, we're at your twelve o'clock', meaning we were at his front. We learned to use the code names.

"In 1st Recon we were outfitted with a pack that weighed from 60 to 80 pounds. We were given a poncho liner, rations, utensils like a fork and cup, fatigues, socks, and a compass and binoculars for the patrol leader or assistant patrol leader.

"We learned the proper radio procedure. Our mission in 1st Recon was to learn to operate in six or nine man groups. We would be told something like 'We anticipate that there's movement at such and such coordinates or grid' and we would be inserted to find out what we could without making any contact with the enemy.

"We learned about claymore mines and what they could do to a whole row of men. Here we were introduced to booby traps, pungi sticks and things like that. We got more first aid training.

"I took the test for jump school. It would have given me another $50.00 if I could have qualified. I took the test where I had to do so many pushups, so many situps and the like, and I came in first. But my vision came out 20/200. I told them the records were wrong. The sergeant said it would take them two months to check everything out and that the whole time I'd be waiting there, probably pulling undesirable duty. 'We want to make sure nobody fails jump school,' he told me. It was provided by the Army so the Marines wanted to make sure nobody that they sent failed. Pride.

"We did a lot of repelling from a tower. We had to go high up on a ladder and then come down on ropes. This was next to the ocean and we had a good view but it was frightening at first to come off that tower. We learned how to handle a raft by paddling together, and it was here that we started hearing Vietnam stories from veterans. These stories made you want to go out and kill, but you never think *they* will kill *you*. At this place we also began to see people who had wife problems, drinking problems.

"I remember we were driving on base one time. I was with two other guys. One of them was this big, dumb guy who was going for sergeant but who overslept in his car and got caught. They lined everybody up to witness it and they took his stripes away from him. He was a *gabacho* (white), a nice guy, but he messed up.

"Another time, he and I and this other guy were driving by in his '62 Ford Falcon. This other guy was driving, and Scoggs (pseudonym) was in the middle, so I decided to play a trick on them. I bent down pretending to be tying my shoe so it looked like the two were sitting close together when we drove by the mess hall. We called him 'Dufus Scoggs' because he was always messing up.

"When we got some time we would go into town and rent a room in a motel. We asked this Black guy where the action was and he showed us a place where the women would come to your room so you could pick the one you wanted. I remember picking a forty-year old woman who told me she made her living in a motel room with the Marines. We tried to save money for every weekend we could because we were rough, tough Marines.

"We heard a lot of stories when we were in the barracks. One guy told us that he had gotten a Bronze Star. It turned out he had had a 2nd degree black belt and sneaked up on three Viet Cong with a knife. He killed one with his bare hands while the second one had died of fright and the third one had run and gotten away.

"There was a Chicano from Harlingen, Texas who had been in Vietnam quite a while. This guy liked to take movie pictures and was a nice guy, always smiling. His name was Abel Perez and I think he was a buck sergeant. He had been in Vietnam twice and he told us decapitation stories that had taken place in 'Nam in '65.

"After I got orders to go to Vietnam, there was one more camp we went to for special Vietnam training. We lived in barracks where everybody was going to Vietnam, so I got pretty used to the idea of going to Vietnam. We learned more about booby traps, had night maneuvers with a compass, and trained to be prisoners of war. They took the food away from you and gave you raw snakes to eat and exercised you until you dropped. They gave you rice. There were more classes and more firing. I was already an expert, though, having gone to North Carolina as a sharpshooter and coming out an expert.

"Our staff sergeant told us we were going to get together with the captain. Basically, the captain told us that some of us were not coming back from Vietnam, so, of course, we all looked around trying to imagine who wasn't coming back, each person thinking, 'I'm coming back, he isn't.'

"When I had to leave, my parents became very upset because they knew what it meant to go where I was going. Especially dad, he was very upset. I remember distinctly that I told them I'd be back.

"I went to Travis Air Force Base, then to Wake Island where we stopped for refueling. We were there one hour, and proceeded to Okinawa, spent one afternoon there, then landed at Kadena, Japan. There we were bussed to Camp Hansen. This place was across from my teacher's (Editor's note: martial arts master Eizo Shimabukuro, with whom Lionel would later develop a close relationship) school. I was supposed to have liberty but didn't get any because they said we might be leaving any time without warning. We got all the shots we needed and some equipment and then we boarded a C-47 at Kadena and flew to Vietnam. I moved over to the side where I could see the hills. There was just the drone of the engines and this beautiful terrain, and I remember thinking, 'This is war?' All I could see was this beautiful red color of the mountains around Da Nang."

Like Discovering Dinosaurs

"We got our billets in Da Nang and they put us immediately to digging trenches because the base was getting rocketed. That first night, this *bolillo* accused me of stealing something.

"This Black guy protected me. He told the other guy to lay off of me because I was new. Then I got my orders to go to Khe Sanh with 3rd Recon. When I got there it was strange. The roaring of planes, helicopters, and the noise of bulldozers working the ground, tearing it up, and the hot, humid air . . . I had expected it to be hot, but not that hot.

"They gave us our tents and assigned us to a platoon. I went on my first patrol after one week, and I was scared. Eight of us went on that patrol. I had a lot to learn, like about the leeches that crawled all over you when you tried to sleep. I had a hard time sleeping, both from not being used to it and because I snored. The other guys would wake me up and I would have to sleep on my side. They couldn't afford to have me snoring when we were trying to hide from the enemy.

"Later on we went on a patrol and had to be extracted by helicopter. We were firing, but I didn't know what the heck was going on till I got back to the base. Turned out we had been followed by NVA (North Vietnamese Army) and I didn't know it.

"After every patrol, we got debriefed. Intelligence would interview us and report everything to headquarters, even if we didn't see anything.

"Normally, we were out four nights and five days. We came back for a week, then we'd go back. They always had reconnaissance patrols out around the base.

"One time we were asked to go inspect this particular hill. The NVA had been there in the trenches. Rations and other evidence of activity indicated that. It was kind of like discovering dinosaurs. It was an awe-inspiring thing, the first time I had seen the work of the enemy, the guys that were really trying to kill me. They did exist. We also found these little green snakes, that were supposed to be very poisonous.

"Most of our time on patrol was peaceful. I had learned to sleep in the side position and didn't snore as much. When we settled in for the night, we had to think about where we would run if the enemy came. Remember, we were a small group, lightly armed, and far away from the other Marines. We set up back to back so that we covered a 180° area or a full circle and we rotated during the night. We always waited, listening for the North

Vietnamese. One night we were waiting like this, it was extremely dark, cold and quiet, and suddenly these lights exploded all over Hill 881 South. We got on the radio and the Marines on 881 hollered, 'Happy New Year!' We had forgotten it was now 1968.

"This was on the same patrol where we heard footsteps around our position. Several times during the night we could hear them circling us, but they didn't find us.

"On another patrol we came across some people that had been hunting. They had killed a black panther. [Editor's note: Probably native Montagnards.)

"Once we were coming down a hill to a creek and were going to be extracted and I heard something. Then I heard a definite noise. 'Sounds like a water buffalo,' I thought.

"Then I heard it again. So we settled down by this creek, peacefully, sitting by our equipment, being cautious, and we heard this noise again. This guy on the patrol always had a camera, an instamatic, and he brought it out right when we heard this 'Rawhhh!' On a rock above us was a Bengal Tiger. He had been following us, and this Black guy's jaw dropped when he saw it. We all aimed our weapons at it, but the tiger only growled again and turned back into the rocks. It had heard the clicks of the instamatic, and that made the tiger turn back.

"For extraction by chopper, we'd call in grid coordinates, then throw smoke grenades to mark our position. Then on the radio, we'd ask the chopper what color he saw. We did it this way because if we told the helicopter pilot the color first, the enemy would throw out the same color and draw the helicopter into a trap.

"Two gunships and C-46 would come in to pick us up in a clearing. The gunships would fly around covering for the C-46 while it picked us up. Sometimes the enemy would open up and the gunships would fire back till we got to our positions. If it was too hot to handle, the C-46 wouldn't land and we had to wait or go to another spot.

"Later on as a civilian I would hear the helicopter blades and think back. And I would think of those blades cutting the air and think of my Sensei who taught me karate in Okinawa, how he taught me to use my hands in the same way, to keep them close to my body just like those two gunships stayed close to the C-46.

"If there was any kind of distraction in Vietnam, like enemy nearby or fog, or rain, they wouldn't pick you up unless it was an emergency.

"On patrol we had a patrol leader and an assistant patrol leader. They would carry a compass and a map. We would carry extra ammo, and some people would carry claymore mines. I carried more rounds for my M-16 and tissue paper. Scotty's was in big demand. It's amazing how important those little things become.

"The can opener was important, just like your ID. These things you kept close to you.

"Leeches crawled on your neck, body, and in your boots. They were *grandotas*, big, and you could see them crawling towards you when you sat down. Everything had to be tight, your blousing on your wrists and ankles had to be closed tight because they would get in even through your *nalgas* (ass cheeks). One guy had to be medevaced with a leech on his penis. It was bleeding and you couldn't apply a tourniquet.

"On Khe Sanh, when we weren't on patrol, we practiced ambushes, night ambushes and day too, and practiced being in position so the NVA wouldn't overrun you.

"The grunts (line infantry) were on Hill 881 South. We never had to pull perimeter guard like they did because we were reconnaissance troops, but we had other duties. Khe Sanh was just building up and we used to get food by parachute. Our job was to guard the food crates from the Montagnard tribesmen. They would rush out when the crates would come down and get crushed by them. They would try to steal the food.

"The planes would come in slow, drop the crates and we would watch them slide with the parachutes till they could be stopped.

"During this time we had outdoor movies on the hill by our positions. I remember 'Road Runner' and 'Alfie'. 'Alfie' was about this guy who had all kinds of women that loved him. I didn't like that movie. All these women loved him and some were married; I didn't like that. Finally, this girl left him.

"When we went somewhere on the base, we congregated only with our platoon. In the first platoon I was in, the Latinos there wouldn't speak Spanish and treated me with suspicion or scorn. They were from California.

"In the second platoon, I was the only Mexican and got along well with Black guys. There were three of them in the platoon.

"We found out that the Air Force was getting better food so we went to steal some. We succeeded. We could always get ham and lima beans, but that time we broke into their supplies and got beef steak.

"We had a limit of two beers per day. They gave you tickets. You could give these tickets away but I used to sell mine and send money to my parents. I kept $10 or $15 for things I needed at the PX (Post Exchange), like cookies, etc.

"We used to tell direction and location by grid sections on the map. We walked two to three miles at a time. We took notes of anything we found, like empty canned goods, anything. It was up to MI (Military Intelligence) to fit everything into a pattern, to look for the enemy. We just put it down in our notebooks, what we found and where.

"Once we were on patrol and had to set up for the night and it rained a lot. Actually, it happened a lot, but this night I was trying to sleep and kept sliding down the hill over and over on the mud.

"For the rain we had plastic pants and jacket and used a canvas cover that we tied from two trees for protection. But we had to be careful to not be too noticeable and give ourselves away. You'd be lying there trying to sleep on the ground, miserable and cold, and the leeches several inches long would come out crawling towards you. They would get in anywhere they could, any place that was exposed, your neck, your nose, your ass if they could.

"If we could burn some tabs and make some coffee, it felt better. A heat tab burned hot and didn't give out a big flame the enemy could see. The warmth made it possible to talk, it helped your teeth to stop chattering from the cold. But you had to be quiet and careful because the rain was a good time for the enemy to attack.

"For breakfast, I always ate date bread. Nobody else liked it and I ate it all with jam whenever I could get it.

"Then we would move out real slow. The point man would carry a rifle and sometimes he would use leather gloves to open a trail when there were a lot of briars and thorns.

"If we needed visibility, somebody would put on some spurs and a belt and climb a tree. A Black guy in our squad could climb really fast, so he would go up and look around so we could get a fix on our position.

"One time we heard noises and thought we were going to get attacked. It turned out *'que eran changos'* -- they were monkeys.

"Another time we were walking on patrol in elephant grass. I was the point man that time and we were moving through a semi-friendly area. I heard this noise, like a truck crashing through the brush, and saw an elephant! It was a work elephant and there were people guiding him. One of them had a long stick. I took a quick glance and didn't fire.

"The people with the elephant wore a lot of old military clothing. These were Montagnard people. Their women wore long dresses. They didn't wear the bamboo hats you saw on tv; those were worn by the Vietnamese to the South.

"Back at Khe Sanh I got to know this Black guy named Diego. He came from Los Angeles, from a broken home. This guy was tall and slender, a good looking Marine who liked to practice karate. This guy was always challenging me to a foot race because he knew he'd win. He'd say, 'Hey, Lionel, you wanna run again?'

"I could never catch up with the guy, but I always replied, 'Sure, I'll beat ya this time.'

"We used to practice karate when we could. I don't know if Diego had severe problems or not. He always talked about his mother, but that's normal 'cause she raised him by herself. One day, Diego told me he had already been in the brig in Da Nang for knifing a *bolillo* (white guy). The *bolillo* had called him some names and Diego had used a bayonet on him.

"We used to practice throwing knives until this *bolillo* from New York broke a couple of them, then the captain said we were ruining them.

"I guess food took on a big importance for me in Vietnam. There was a ritual about the whole thing when we were out there in the mud and rain for a whole week. We used to put some holes in a can and put it over a heat tab for making coffee. Empty cans of the fruit cocktail were the best for making coffee because you could rinse them out easy. It was a larger can too. We would fold back the lid and use that as a handle while holding it over the flame of the heat tab. I would put some coffee in there and some sugar and chocolate and heat it up, and I'd have it with my date bread. Sometimes we had eggs.

"Later on we got better food in aluminum packs. You just heated the water and put the food in there. We got spaghetti and hot sauce this way.

"Sometimes we got bad food; you had to be careful. Some people at Khe Sanh got *gusanos* (worms) and had to be dewormed.

"Our patrols often took us through elephant grass. It looked pretty tall but sometimes it wasn't, especially higher up in the mountains. One time I jumped from the chopper thinking I was close to the ground. The pilot saw me disappear and had to lower the chopper quite a bit so the others who had to jump didn't have to take the same fall. The grass just swallowed me up and I hit hard."

In a Field of Elephant Grass

"Getting accepted at Khe Sanh was just like anything else. You had to feel things out. It's when people go in with the attitude that they know everything that they run into problems. Just to give you an idea of what I mean is this guy who thought he knew everything about Blacks. He was trying to be Mr. Cool. I remember we were playing cards that night and he was saying he knew all the places to go and he knew this and that. He came across as pretty stinko. Anyway, Mr. Cool had to leave the place for a while and while he was gone, this other guy that was drinking beer pissed in a bottle. When Mr. Cool came back the guy handed him the bottle, and Mr. Cool drank it and said, 'Ah, that's good!' Then they laughed and told him it was urine mixed with beer. It was a guy named Burnette (pseudonym) that urinated in the bottle. He was a crazy guy.

"There was this other guy that was in the same platoon but a different tent. He had written home to his girlfriend and had indicated that all the Marines had an IQ of 90. He was a college graduate and he was a selfish guy.

"He was just a private. Somehow one of the people got to read the letter. He had left it out in the open and everybody found out about it. He was kind of a hippie guy, always playing the Beatles on his tape recorder. He was a Beatles fan, 'Love you, yeah, yeah, yeah!'

"This guy was a pain in the neck. One time we were out in the field, about seven of us, and he was our radio man; he was sort of on point. When we stopped, instead of being on guard, we found him reading a book. This was out in the field, and remember this was a tiny recon unit. He may have been sharp but he lacked some common sense.

"Another time we were out in the field in the elephant grass. There was a slight hill and we slept there that night. Then it started raining, I mean really raining. So what does this guy do in the middle of the night? He creeps up forward! It was wet where he was sleeping, so in the middle of the night, he moved after he finished his guard. We didn't know where he was. We heard the noise and we woke everybody up by hand. Everybody had their rifles up ready to go. We heard this noise and practically everybody was ready. As it turned out it was this same guy. He had moved because it was wet at his location. We're talking about a few feet but that makes a lot of difference. Five or six feet. (Editor's note: This is a recurring item of the Vietnam experience, as revealed by combat veterans. Moving a few feet could get you killed. Being where you were supposed to be was important, too, if you expected to get accurate artillery support. However, later on in the war, being where you were supposed to be was at times perceived as going out on useless missions in a war that was already considered lost by the public.)

"You were all ears at night because you slept pretty close together. I remember when I first got there ... we were out in the bush and I was sleeping. It was a forest type of terrain there. They said I was snoring a lot and that in one particular instance I stood up and said something out loud. I yelled in my sleep.

"There were a lot of times that I couldn't sleep because I would snore. They kept waking me up because sound travels. Then when I first started leading patrols I couldn't sleep. I would sit up just thinking and only sleep a few hours. I would be thinking about the people, thinking about my mission . . . everything.

"It was about four months before I led my own patrol. Kalama (the Hawaiian) was my first guide; I used to go on patrols with him. He's the one that taught me what I needed to know. He was my guide, so when I first went on patrol he was there with me to help me out. He was pretty good, he was a teacher, a mentor. He had been there for quite a while.

"I remember this guy from Guatemala. He didn't have much time left in Vietnam. Right before he was ready to go back to Guatemala, he got into a firefight. It was a big firefight. Anyway, they were extracted and we were inserted into the area where they had been. Because of the firefight, he got the Navy Cross--but there were some questions. Some people say that it was a faked firefight because he wanted to get back home, and that everything had been well planned out ahead of time. Just about everybody got a medal there.

"Everybody in the squad was a short-timer and once you reach that point, you're ready to go back home. They could well have done what they said they did. When you get back from a mission you get interrogated to make sure everybody is telling the truth. But we had been in that area and we didn't get anything. Then they went in and they got into a big firefight in that same area and they saw--I forgot how many people (enemy)--but nobody got hurt. Then we were inserted into the same area after they got out. And we couldn't find anything.

"But I'll never forget, he (the Guatemalan) was given the Navy Cross and other people got the Bronze Star, and other decorations. I remember the ceremony. Burnette was there. He got the Bronze Star. It's just like anything. It seemed like it was a lot of politics.

"I also remember that this crazy guy from New York was our patrol leader. We had gone through Basic together. At Khe Sanh he was in a position on ambush and one of the guys saw something moving and this guy just aimed his rifle and shot an NVA soldier through the head. He didn't care if he gave away our position. He got two of them. Later on he said, 'Guerra, I got my first kill. When are you going to get yours?'

Hill 881 North

"We detected enemy activity on Hill 881 North, so we sent a patrol up there to collect information and to set up an ambush, but they got ambushed instead. The officers didn't let me go on that patrol.

"Three got killed, the point, the second and a lieutenant. At that point I started getting hatred. Goose pimples just crawled on my skin.

"We went to the helipad to help them when they brought them in. My friend, *el negrito*, Diego, was wounded. He's the one I used to run foot races with. Before he was always smiling, and now he was hit in the groin and near the heart. I started swearing and I had never sworn before. I grabbed his hand; it was dangling. It really tore me apart inside. Later on he passed away. The hardest part was that you had to pack his things to get ready to send home. (Editor's Note: Lionel Guerra discovered in 1985 that Diego had survived!)

"So, our own mission became to get a radio that was left up there by the patrol that was ambushed, and to get some information. The night before, we were put on a helicopter at Khe Sanh and taken to the Hill 881 North, to the hill base. That night we went over our plans. The platoon leaders and squad leaders met with the Infantry people that were going to lead us up and with the captain, too. We had the plan and everything. I'll never forget this guy that I met that night. He was going to be the point man for our direction.

"The following morning, we left at four or five. It was still dark but beginning to get light. It was really foggy, you couldn't see in front of you. We went out with grunts, the Infantry people. I think there were 150 of us.

"One string of people left in one direction and another string left in the other direction. We had cover for both sides of the hill. At this time we were not assaulting, we were just going to the hill. As we were moving on the trail, the point man was hit. By accident we had run into the enemy camp! They were dug in and they just hit us right there. The seven of us in the Recon unit were quite a ways back in the line when the people in front got hit.

"Our mission had been to get the radio and if we made contact, we were to come back with the radio if we could. If we didn't make contact, the Recon unit was supposed to stay there. So when we got hit we knew we were going to leave because we had made contact. We retreated and got the wounded out.

"We called in some artillery and also the helicopters to get the wounded out. Then we shot the M-79 grenade launchers at the hill. We had gotten hit on both sides. It was chaotic and there was a lot of confusion. There's always confusion. The guy that got hit . . . he died. He was the same guy I had met on the hill the night before, the point man.

"For a while we traded fire with the NVA, firing M-79's and M-16 fire, then after a while, we assaulted. I remember there were guys crying that didn't want to go. I pushed one of them and hollered at him, 'Get your ass out there!'

"As we moved up in a line, I turned and saw the captain standing watching us, and the base Marines yelling. They could see everything from the sandbags. We had been trained as scouts, to sneak around and gather information, but here we were attacking in line right up the hill. We weren't trained to fight that way, but we fixed bayonets and moved up anyway.

"As we were going up the hill the radio man and I got wounded. I spun around and saw my arm stretched out twisted, with blood oozing out. I grabbed my arm and put a bandage on it. Quickly, the radio man got hit in the leg. He was an Italian, Peralta, and his shin was split open. That's when the corporal started yelling for me to get on the radio. I was going to help the radio man. I was on one side and tried to help him. As I was going to help him, there was a blast from a grenade and I was wounded again.

"There was mass confusion. We thought that our own troops were firing at us, too. We were too close. We thought the other people got in first (to the top of the hill in a pincer movement) and began firing at us. I think that's the reason we wanted to call the people on the radio to stop the firing. But, we knew there were NVA there also, without a doubt.

"We felt a suspicion and started yelling for them to stop shooting. I couldn't help the radio man because I was wounded too, and the patrol leader was yelling at me to help him. The elephant grass kept us hidden, but the sniper rounds came inches over our heads. This Black Marine was crawling around and yelled at us to get in order, and we thought he was crazy. The patrol leader yelled at me to help the radio man, and then he ordered me to get to the radio and call base.

"About this time I moved to the radio but as I did this a grenade landed and got me in the rear and legs. Finally, the patrol leader stood up and ran to help the radio man and got shot and killed immediately.

"After we were wounded, we got our people together and retreated to a safer area. One guy next to me got hit. It just went 'thwwatch!' It was a sniper that got him. We had crawled back to a safety area where the helicopter was landing to remove the wounded. We were there lying down and the bullets were coming in. 'Zoeeeeoooom! Zheeeeoooom!'

"The guy that got hit was one of the guys in my squad. He got hit in the back of the leg ... 'Ppfuuoot!' You could hear it. We were getting shot at from the top down and we were also getting sniper fire. They were all around us.

"Things got pretty hairy. One of our helicopters got shot down but nobody was hurt. Then another helicopter came in to pick us up. There was blood all over the place; some people were dying. The crewman asked me how the other people were doing and I said it like I knew it to be: 'They were killed.'

"They took us back to Khe Sanh base. The first thing they did was offer me a cigarette. I was all bandaged up, and they said it was so I wouldn't bleed to death. We were in a large tent. It was open and you could see all the wounded people in there on stretchers. I could walk so I thought I was ok but they made me lie down on a stretcher and stripped me. Then they put us on a C-47 (plane) with other wounded Marines and took us to Da Nang. I had surgery right away on a hospital ship the U.S.S. Sanctuary. It was *escurito* (dark) but I could see the reflection of the water and hear the helicopter blades.

"The captain who was going to operate on me said, 'You sure came at the right time. You interrupted my favorite tv program.'

"Another guy said, 'Thank God they didn't hit you down there.' I had taken shrapnel in the legs but it didn't hit any vital organs.

"The doctor asked me to move my arm. He told me not to think about the pain. The next thing I knew I had awakened with my arm in a cast with steel rods holding me down. I asked the doctor when I was going to get out because I didn't like being tied down.

"A Vietnamese down the hall was having his legs amputated and we could hear his screams. Next to my bunk there was a sergeant who had gotten sick, but he wasn't wounded. He used to talk to me, to try to help me. I would go to sleep on him, just drift off.

"To get a better perspective, you should read the book I bought on Khe Sanh. It's a thick book and gives you a good idea of the terrain. After I was wounded they assaulted again and they took over the hill. I read about it later in the Stars and Stripes."

Chapter Thirteen

They Knew It Destroyed Us Inside

Don Neptune
1970-71
Medevacs

"It's taken me a long time to go through a lot of things in my life and a lot of people don't understand about Vietnam veterans, that we sacrificed a lot." Don Neptune, Medic, U.S. Army

Mission at Phang Rang: Pilot Panicked
A Macabre Grin
Could You Take My Baby to the United States?
Mary Ann
The Doctor Froze
The Wounded from Cambodia
Throwing Out the Dead
The Children as Shields
An Overdose
Bible in my Zipper Pocket
A Miracle

Note from Editor: Don Neptune is not a Chicano, but he is a friend. More importantly, he had a significant story to tell. A passionate story.

Mission at Phang Rang: Pilot Panicked

"It was a Sunday morning and a helicopter from our unit had a mission. It was called an 'urgent hoist mission'. It was about 3 klics (kilometers) due northeast of Phang Rang. What took place is that as the helicopter was making an approach into the LZ (Landing Zone), they started taking fire and the helicopter was shot up really bad. They made it back in. We watched it come back in. It was streaming smoke.

"They landed and shut down, and one of the pilots who had only been in our company for about a week--he jumped down on his knees and he was crying. I would have been crying too, anybody would have been. He had taken a round right in his helmet and it spun around and went out the top of the greenhouse. It melted into that Bell helicopter about half an inch. The round did, it just left a groove around the top of it, there in a circle.

"The helicopter had about six rounds through the transmission and all the windows were blown out. All the cargo door windows were blown out: they were pinned back anyway. It had I don't know how many rounds went through the rotor blades. All of the bubbles were blown out, the greenhouses, the windshields were blown . . .

"It had been about three klics away, had tried to make it into the LZ, and never made it in. They were coming in on an approach and they never made it. They came back and they told me and my crew chief to get ready to go because their helicopter hadn't gone into maintenance yet. So we just went out to our bird and got in and took off for the LZ. It was called in as a 'hoist mission' but it was anything but a hoist mission.

"It was in the middle of a rice paddy with tree lines spurring out along the rice paddies. When we came in, we were taking fire, machine gun fire ... we couldn't really pinpoint where the fire was coming from. It was just from the tree lines. It was kind of windy that day and we could see some people on the ground.

"It was daylight but I could see muzzle flashes in the tree line. There were people on the ground pinned down. It was mainly a Vietnamese platoon with some American Rangers. When we came down, my crew chief jumped out and I jumped out and we ran in opposite directions. We saw the wounded, and I picked up a man and my crew chief picked up a man. They were about fifty yards from the helicopter. We ran back and threw them on the helicopter. Our pilots were shooting their machine guns out the windows.

"I turned around and I was running towards three guys. I had just about got to them and this guy jumps out, it was a Ranger who jumped up and grabbed my arm. I didn't even see him there for a moment, and he pulled me down to the ground. He told me that those guys were dead, the ones that I was running to. So I said, 'We got to get the wounded together'--and about that time I saw my crew chief running for the helicopter. I told him, this sergeant, I don't know what unit he was from (he was a Black guy), and he said, 'Ok,' he'd try to get his wounded together.

"I started to run back towards the helicopter and the pilot was shootin' his machinegun out the window. My crew chief had another wounded guy; he was carryin' him. They flew off and left us . . . we didn't understand the reason why.

"I went back with the Ranger and we started gettin' the wounded together. But there was too much machinegun fire so we were kinda pinned down. So we didn't do anything at that time. My crew chief was separated from me, and we were too far apart and we weren't gonna move to each other. Then the helicopter came back in. I couldn't say how long a period of time it was till it came back, it might have been fifteen minutes, maybe less. In that kind of a situation time is kind of irrelevant . . . distorted. But it seemed like a long time.

"They came back in but they didn't slow down other than for us to jump onto the skids. We were hanging onto the skids and my crew chief was holding on . . . he had this guy and had him holding on with one hand to the skid and with the other hand he had this guy about the ankle. I crawled over to the other side and I grabbed his hand. I couldn't pull both of them in, so he had to make a decision. He let the guy go . . . he was a Vietnamese.

"My crew chief pulled his .38 and he told the pilots they didn't have to worry about the enemy shootin' 'em down. If they ever left him and his medic again like that, that they wouldn't have to worry about the enemy. He knocked 'em around the side of the head; they had their helmets on, but he kind of hit 'em ... with his .38. They were cryin' and apologizing. It was a bad scene. So they asked us what we wanted to do and we said we weren't gonna go back unless we had some gunship protection. So they called out a couple of . . . I remember seeing two Cobra gunships and I saw an F-4 fighter come in real low right next to us. We were about fifteen feet off the ground in the helicopter coming in again.

"This Ranger had all these wounded ready to go. They were stacked up ready to go. We just hovered there and threw them on and took off for Cam Rahn Bay to the hospital. That's about all I can remember."

A Macabre Grin

"We picked up seventeen dead guys--Vietnamese. We picked them up near Da Lat up in the mountains. They had been out in the jungle for about three days. We normally didn't go up and pick up dead people. We normally just picked up wounded.

"What happened was we picked 'em up and we were flying back in to Da Lat, and we started talkin' about how the smell was gettin' pretty bad. We thought it would be kind of humorous for the guys who were going to come and pick 'em up, that were going to help us unload these dead, to make it a little interesting. So what we did was ... we usually flew with our doors pinned back, and we decided to close our cargo doors. So we just kind of closed our cargo doors and looked at each other in a macabre grin. We just kind of sat there.

"When we landed at Da Lat, we saw all these guys ready to help us unload these dead guys. They were just really eager. So when we landed, it was really a nice day and it was at this big lake they had up there, it was a nice resort type of a little town. Yeah, they knew these guys we had picked up were dead or wounded or whatever--they were quite dead. We had 'em stacked in there like cordwood. It was very gross. It smelled a lot. They were shot up and bloated and all. Rigor mortis had set in and all their eyes were open. That's the way people die, I mean when somebody dies, whatever position they're in that's the way, that's the form they take. They kind of draw up into a fetal position.

"Anyway, the first three guys *ran* for the helicopter to help us unload 'em. And just as they about reached the door, I opened the cargo door and swung it open, back open. They hit the ground. The smell rolled out of there and just hit 'em and it just knocked 'em out! And the next six guys, they were about fifteen feet back, they just started retching, *just* uncontrollable.

"We were used to this. We just kind of laughed, and we unloaded 'em and flew off. It was kind of strange, but that was one of the ways to keep our sanity without going too crazy.

"It was a job that had to be done. We weren't being disrespectful to the dead. They were dead.

Editor's Note: At this point in the interview, Don's wife interjects: "I think it kind of helped the people that were on the ground, too . . . to remember what these guys were going through.

Don's wife continues, "Was that a dream or did that really happen when you were in the helicopter and with all the eyes looking at you? Was that a dream? One of your nightmares?"

Don replies, "Oh, yeah, that was a dream I used to have."

Interviewer asks, "Back stateside?"

Don, "Yeah."

"When you were finishing out your tour?"

Don, "Dead and wounded. Their eyes staring out at me. Just dreams that I had."

Could You Take My Baby to the United States?

"We used to fly out of a little Navy compound out in the middle of nowhere. It was at a place called Bao Loc. There was a big bazaar there in the village where they used to sell silk and . . . it was a marketplace and quite interesting. We'd go down to the bazaar and take radios with us in case we got called for a mission so we could get right back.

"I was at this little bazaar one day with my crew chief, and a woman came up to me with a ... maybe . . . a year-and-a-half to two-year old little girl. She had blond hair and blue eyes and she had gold earrings, pierced earrings. The mother was saying, 'Could you take my baby back to the United States?'"

Don's wife speaks up, "Don and I have thought about it . . ."

Don, "I would have liked to have taken that baby."

Don's wife continues, "If there was any way, if she was in an orphanage or something and we could get in touch ... We'd love to ... find her. 'Cause that little girl has been on his mind all these years."

Don, "But there was no way I could take her because I was flying combat missions. That's where I was. We were at Bao Loc and we used to fly combat missions out of Bao Loc."

Mary Ann

"I was at Chu Lai in the hospital and I had some sort of jungle fever or malaria. It was never determined but I . . . was very ill. They were giving me quinine; they were treatin' it like malaria.

"I had a real high fever. When I was in the hospital ward there was just one guy across from me and there were just . . . I can't remember how many beds there were in there. But there was this one guy in there, he had been with an armored car unit up on the DMZ. I can't remember his name. His fingers were burned from being inside a Duster at Dong Ha. He's across from me and I'm talkin' to 'im.

"That night I woke up and it was wall to wall beds. And what woke me up was guys moanin' and kind of screaming out. What had happened is they pulled out all their big guns from Mary Ann, which is a firebase next to Chu Lai. They were gettin' ready to stand down. They pulled out all their big guns first. So they didn't have the support when the enemy attacked. This is what this one guy was tellin' me; they hit them with about eighty rounds of mortars, and about forty of gas, and they came in wearing gas masks. And they cut down our flag and raised theirs, and they were gone before the morning and there was only one guy that wasn't wounded and he was the guy that had a bunker collapse down around 'im. But everybody else was either wounded or killed. I don't remember how many guys were in that firebase, but I think there were over a hundred guys there."

The Doctor Froze

"When I first got in-country I went to Cu Chi and worked as a corpsman at the 12th Evac Hospital there. The first guy I worked on was shot from head to toe. He was an NVA and had green canvas tennis shoes. Boots, kind of canvas boots. He had been shot from head to toe with an M-16.

"He was screamin'. They had just brought him in off the helicopter. It was early in the morning and they brought this guy in and right after that, they brought in four Americans who were shot by their own men. That's why I can remember it so vividly, because it was my first day there.

"They had been forward observers for their company and they got off course. Their company got off course and came up on 'em. The four guys were sittin' underneath a tree. They were eatin' and the company opened up on 'em. They tried fightin' 'em at first but they were way outnumbered. They didn't know who it was at first. They thought it was the enemy and then they realized it was their own company because of the weapons they were using. They tried swimming across the river, that's where they got shot. It was a small river.

"One guy was shot in the back and he was dyin'. But he lived. They were all shot running away. One guy was shot in the buttocks, another guy was shot in the thigh, another guy was shot in the arm.

"This guy, he remembered . . . he was looking at me and he was screaming, 'God, help me!' and he was drownin' in his own blood. There was a doctor who was workin' on 'im and he was gettin' ready to open 'im up and he just froze and turned white. This other doctor came up and he said, 'If you don't know what you're doing, just get out of the way!' and he pushed him out of the way. This second doctor just went sshhhpp! and ripped him open (the patient), shoved a chest tube in him, and saved that guy's life. They drained him ... and took the bullet out.

"A few days later he asked to see me because I was the last person he saw going in and he wanted to thank me. I had been praying for him right then when they operated on him. He didn't know I was praying for him, but I was looking him right in the eyes and I was praying for him.

The Wounded from Cambodia

"I was at Cu Chi for about a month and a half. Then they asked for volunteers for Dustoff medevac (combat medical helicopter). You had to volunteer for it. They just didn't take you and put you in it. So I volunteered for medevac. The guy in the orderly room there at headquarters looked at us kind of strange. He said, 'You're crazy for doing this. It's really a dangerous job.' He looked at us kind of strange. There were just two of us that volunteered. The guy just kind of shook his head and said, 'You guys don't know what you're gettin' yourselves into.'

"The life expectancy for a medevac, he told us, was the same as for a radio man or a machine-gunner, somewhere around in there--eleven seconds in combat.

"I figured it was gonna be pretty rough but that was my choice at the time. It was just a decision that I made. I felt good about it.

"The 12th Evac Hospital, while I worked there, I worked with some real wonderful nurses. The nurses, the other medics, and some doctors there were really excellent people.

"Cu Chi was a big firebase. It was quite busy for us there all the time, a lot of work. We got a lot of wounded that first month. They were coming out of that fighting along the Cambodian border. We had so many wounded at one time that we couldn't send the really badly wounded off to Japan or to the hospital ship. We couldn't get 'em out of there. They had to stay maybe two or three weeks. We tried to get them out as soon as possible because Medevacs were constantly bringing in more wounded every day.

"When I left Cu Chi, a helicopter from my new unit came to pick me up. I was standing out there with my bag by the helipad and they landed and said 'Get on.'

"The sergeant looked at me and said, 'You'll never make it.' This sergeant left after about two months of my gettin' there. He was an old-timer. He'd been in for almost thirty years and he was gettin' out. But he was a good man, he was a good medic.

"On my first day I was with my unit, they had given me a bunk and a hootch. I was with this other guy. We were kinda just hangin' around, there wasn't much goin' on, and I heard some music comin' from a hootch next to mine. I thought I'd just go over and kinda introduce myself to some of the people in the unit there. I walked into this hootch and there was a long hallway and it had beads and runners down this hallway that you had to go through.

"There were rooms all the way down . . . and when you walked through these beads and streamers the Vietnamese sold, you kind of parted your way through them. I walked down in there and there was an open bay in the back, and there was music blasting out. Some guy had a tape deck back there and loud rock 'n roll music was playin'.

"There was a footlocker out there in the middle of the bay and it had a *big* pile of marijuana on it . . . about a foot high on top of this footlocker. There was a guy sittin' in a chair with a gas mask on and a pipe stickin' out of it. There was another guy that was hangin' on to a cord that mamasan used to hang clothes on. He had a bottle of whiskey in one hand and a joint in the other hand and he was hangin' on to this cord, and he was yellin', 'How do ya get off this train?' He was pretty wiped out.

"The next thing I knew, I had a forty-five pointed at my head and a M-79 grenade launcher up against my chin. They had grabbed a t-shirt or somethin' and put it around my throat from behind and had me around one of those big beams. They were chokin' me and wanted to know who I was, where I was from . . .

"They kind of interrogated me for maybe around twenty or thirty minutes. They wanted to make sure . . . they didn't know who I was. Probably they didn't care really. I think they were more or less just being themselves. I don't know. Probably they wanted to make sure I wasn't an informer.

"I told 'em I was the new medic for the company, and a couple of the medics said, 'Hey, let 'im go, he's my replacement!' And another guy said, 'No! He's *my* replacement!' And pretty soon there was two or three medics fightin' over whose replacement I was. They were all pretty short (Editor: meaning few days left in tour), so one of them took me under his wing, and his name was Charlie Martinez.

"The purpose of the Medevac at Phang Rang was to cover II Corps, approximately twenty thousand square miles. We picked up all the wounded within that range. We had different firebases that we worked out of. We had six helicopters in our unit.

"I'm sure that other gunships picked up the wounded if they were there, but we picked up most of the infantry wounded. We would call for gunship escorts if they could give us escort, but a lot of times they couldn't.

"All the pilots in one unit would switch off helicopters. We had a crew chief who stayed on a bird, and a medic who also stayed with one bird. That was their helicopter and they stayed with it. The helicopters had different names to them. Every crew chief could name his helicopter and they'd paint it on the front.

"One of the helicopters in our unit was named 'Proud Mary', we had one called 'Jungle Bunny', we had another one called 'So Others May Live'. Ours was called 'The Paddy Dasher'.

"We flew out of Phang Rang, and a place called Whiskey Mountain, down around Phon Tiet. We flew out of Nha Trang, and a place called Boa Loc. Those were the four places we would fly missions out of. The helicopter would go up there for maybe three or four weeks to a month. Maybe two months, a month and a half. We would fly missions out of there.

"A lot of times another helicopter would be sent up to meet them half way to a hospital and it would transport the wounded to the hospital and then the original helicopter would stay at that firebase and work out of that firebase. You're flying a lot of hours, a lot of missions, day and night.

"Phang Rang was a tactical fighter base and was pretty secure. Whiskey Mountain was at a little engineer firebase. It was kind of isolated, in the middle of nowhere.

"We were always on call to go. We had 'first, second, and third up'. Back in the rear we had three helicopters on standby. It was always first, second and third up. First up would take all the first missions coming in. If first up couldn't get all missions coming in, then second up would go and take those missions. So you were always on call and had to stay ready all the time.

"We flew at night through thunderstorms. We had night-hoist missions. They had a jungle penetrator in which you loaded the wounded, and then you'd hoist 'em up. Then they'd bring the medic up separately. They could take up to three wounded at one time. Usually they would just strap two guys on.

"I've been in over three hundred missions. I saw everything. I saw people with three head wounds, one that lost part of his butt and had a leg blown off. But you just go on. I've had tracers next to my face, running on the ground, or in the chopper. Once a green tracer was coming at me, I saw it, I was looking down and suddenly this green tracer was coming right for me and veered off, went right by my nose.

"One time I flew this Vietnamese boy one hundred miles to get him to a hospital where they could save his life. When we got there they told me they weren't treating Vietnamese any more. 'Get that kid out of here' the doctor yelled.

"I argued with them that the kid had been hit by an American truck and it was our responsibility to take care of him. The doctor began to cuss me out.

"The kid had a hematoma, and had a fractured skull with fluid leaking out. It really pissed me off. I told the doctor on duty, 'If you don't take care of that kid, you're not going to see the sun rise!' And I meant it. I had a forty-five, ready and cocked. What could they have done to me? What could they have done to me that was worse than what I was already going through? They had a hard time finding replacement medics. We were all volunteers.

"We're going into an LZ and we had this Vietnamese radio man from a Vietnamese unit on the ground and he wasn't making it. He was popping smoke on the ground, but real lethargic. We didn't want to get shot, so I threw open the back door and threatened to throw him out. You know, they lived in it day in and day out. They had had it with fighting the war. They needed a shaking out now and then.

"He was telling them to pop smoke. But from the ground we were gettin' all different kinds of smoke.

"He couldn't find the right LZ. They were poppin' smoke here, poppin' smoke here, poppin' smoke a half a mile away. So I was trying to get him to pop different colors of smoke to verify the right LZ. But nothing was happening. So finally he got a hold of them on the ground and he told me, 'That's all they have is white smoke.'

"And I said, 'Pop double white smoke in succession.' So they did. But basically, it was trying to get everything squared away because we wouldn't fly down there if we were going to be ambushed.

Throwing Out the Dead

"I was throwing out the dead to make room for the wounded. This Vietnamese on the ground almost shot me 'cause I threw out the dead. He took offense. I don't know . . . maybe those were his friends or relatives. The last time I saw him a captain had jumped out of the trench and pointed a .45 at him. He was trying to get me sighted in, had an M-16 pointed at me. I could see him pointing, sighting in, I could see him, he was bouncing as the helicopter moved. It made it look like he was bouncing. I was standing on the skids and wanted to get away fast. I yelled at the captain, 'He's trying to take me out!'--and the captain banked the helicopter to throw off his aim.

"You've got to remember the Vietnamese are into ancestor worship. Maybe that had something to do with it. He took offense at my throwing out the dead. We had to take the wounded, they were still bringing in the wounded.

"Another time, I threw out this U.S. major that wouldn't make room on the helicopter for his wounded men. I just grabbed him and pushed him off. We were on a mountain top, near Da Lat, in an overweight helicopter. Too much cargo. We started to rise but then ran into trouble because the air got thinner the higher we went. We were already on a mountain top. It made it harder to get any lift. We had a hell of a time just clearing the pine trees."

The Children As Shields

"We had a pilot, a CW4 snorting heroin. They did it because sometimes that was the only way you could keep your sanity. That was the only way you could keep going back mission after mission. We found out, and I thought of putting a gun to his head, I mean we were pissed. 'I don't want you nodding off on me. You're gonna let the co-pilot fly this time.'

"One time I picked up a ground medic, a guy who served with the grunts. He wanted to go up to see what it was like and it was a night mission. I told him, 'Whatever you do, don't look around.' But he went into shock. He just wasn't used to being in the open like that with nowhere to hide. I couldn't help him. Up in a chopper you don't have anywhere to hide.

"A lot of things that happened over there were hard to cope with. The 1st Infantry Division had to fight NVA who used women and children as shields. They knew it really destroyed us inside because we were Americans, and Americans hate to shoot women and children. I had a friend, a machine gunner, who finally just quit. He couldn't stand to shoot women and children anymore.

"We came back to our base camp after being 67 days in the field and our lockers had been broken into and looted. It pissed you off. Nobody cared.

"My crew chief finally quit after eleven months. He just couldn't take it anymore. I myself went on over three hundred missions. I saw everything. I used to be quiet, real religious, but when I got there I started to lose a lot of weight. We worked eighteen-hour days and had a lot of helicopters shot up. We had more hours than anybody on our chopper. The pilots didn't have confidence in the chief but I knew he was the best crew chief around. We went through a lot. I worked on a guy with his arms and legs blown off and his brains hanging out. He pleaded with me, 'Don't work on me! Let me die!' But we had to try.

"We caught two men back at our base camp who became junkies. We caught them, it wasn't hard. They'd be nodding off. We took their responsibilities away from them. They had tried to break into our medical bags to get the needles and steal our morphine. These guys were beyond smoking dope or snorting heroin. They were mainlining.

"We didn't have to take any shit off anybody because of what we went through. We were going to hang our supply sergeant. He locked the door on us. There were eight to nine of us; we took an axe to the door. He got on his knees and was begging for his life. He had sold our rations, just left us with the bad rations. We told him the next time it would be his life; we had the rope around him and over a crossbeam. After that we broke into supply and got whatever we wanted. But he still couldn't get us our rations. We were still stuck with 1950s c-rations for three months. I mean, we were pissed. He was on his knees begging for his life. We already had the noose around his neck.

"You know, I can tell in the first five minutes if a veteran's been in combat. We went through a lot. After throwing out the dead like I did, to make room for the wounded, everything else seems small by comparison. Civilian life seems boring after that."

An Overdose

"This other incident happened late in my tour at Phang Rang. One night I woke up for some unknown reason. I got up and started walkin' around, it was about four in the morning, and I went by this one hootch and there was this guy lying there. He was a medic and he had one day left to go. He was lying there and he had a needle in his arm and bile was coming out of his mouth. I went and got this other medic and we came down and started popping ammonia nitrate capsules in his nose and giving him CPR and brought him back to life.

"But the first sergeant and the CO had found him like that. They had gone over to the orderly room and started writing up court martial papers on him. They didn't even offer to help him or anything. This guy was *dead*. He was dead when we found him. His heart had stopped and he wasn't breathing.

"But there was another time when these two junkies were fighting. This one guy was choking this other one. The one being choked was almost unconscious, and the fight occurred because one of them wore the other guy's flip-flops, shower shoes.

"Everybody knew these guys were the ones ripping off the needles. Everybody in our company knew. They just didn't give them any responsibilities. Nobody treated 'em real bad . . .

"These guys didn't get court martialled because at that time they had an amnesty program going on over there. In the case of the earlier guy, the one we found on an overdose, rather than court-martial and flag his orders they weren't worried about it, they were just gonna send 'im on and let him get caught at Cam Rahn. So they just let him go. They dropped it because they knew he was going to get caught up there. That's when they had set up the 6th CC, where you had to piss into a bottle before you went home.

"It was real bad over there as far as alcohol and barbiturates. It was the year between 1970 and 71. There was a big heroin epidemic over there. It was getting really bad. Before it seemed like there was just a lot of marijuana usage. Now it was turning into major heroin distribution everywhere. Guys were using heroin.

"At ten months when I was over there, we'd be flying out on a mission without having picked up anybody yet . . . and at times I'd see people floating around. Dead bodies floatin' around just like I'm sittin' here lookin' at you. I wouldn't be . . . it wasn't a dream or anything. But it seemed like it was a dream.

"But I asked about it. Back in the rear I went to see a doctor to see what that was about. He said it was perfectly normal for the type of work that we were doing, and he said it was just the subconscious releasing things that we had seen and had been repressed. They were things the mind had blocked out, that would just be coming back. That just happened a few times. But it was like really real; it was like I was awake. My eyes were open.

Bible in My Zipper Pocket

"I used to carry a Bible. It was a whole Bible, a small Bible. I used to carry it on my thigh, you know the nomacs had zipper pockets. I used to carry it there. It was a flight suit. What it was ... was that it could withstand flash fires.

"I had this Bible and when I was getting ready to leave my unit, this guy came up to me with a request. He flew as a patient protector, as an extra gunner, and he also worked in supply. He would go up in the helicopter with me sometimes. He was one of the only ones who would go up and fly as an extra gunner, as a patient protector. His name was James Johnson. Right before I left Vietnam, it was kind of a custom in our unit to give stuff away if you weren't taking it home with you. He pulled me aside right before I was leaving and he asked me if he could have something of mine. I said, 'Sure, you name it, you got it.'

"And he said, 'Could I have your Bible?' It was the hardest thing I ever had to part with in my whole life, but I said, 'Sure.' I gave him my Bible. I figured he needed it because he had six months more to go. So I gave him my Bible."

A Miracle

"I kind of felt bad about leaving when I came back to the States. I kind of wanted to be back over there with my unit. I felt like part of me was missing. I felt like (over there) at least I knew where I stood. When I came back, I was still in the service. They gave me thirty days and I took leave. But my days on leave were strange. I mainly stayed by myself. I came home to West Richland. I just kind of stayed by myself, just kind of relaxed. It was kind of difficult to talk to people.

"Then I went to Fort Stewart, Georgia. I was in a helicopter unit called the 498th. It was another medevac unit. They made me a senior flight medic. We were meeting medevac planes coming back from Vietnam. We would help pick people off the medevac birds and fly them into the hospital there.

"At Fort Stewart, we flew medevac for Military Assistance, Safety, and Traffic. We would pick up Saturday night barroom casualties and traffic accident victims and fly them to the different hospitals. Or we would transfer patients from one hospital to another. It was military assistance to the civilian population.

"We had two corpsmen, infantry corpsmen. I saw stress in both of them, a lot of stress. And on the other crew chiefs that flew gunships, too. It was a small unit. There were only eight or ten of us who had been to Vietnam. Most of the pilots there had never been to Vietnam. Most of them were straight out of flight school.

"For about six months, we did nothing because we had nothing to do. There were no pilots there. It was just us who had come out of Vietnam. We'd play poker and drink. I started having dreams of bodies floating around. I could see the dead guys in the same room with me.

"At the helicopter they took my picture for a . . . I didn't even know what it was for . . . but when I was flying back from Fort Stewart, I saw myself next to my helicopter with my helmet on. It was an army recruiting poster. They had never told me what it was for, a recruiting picture. I just saw it.

"I went over as a Christian, Full Gospel. And when I came back, I still believed in the Lord, even though you see all the destruction and death. Some people blame the Lord, but it's man's problem. And nobody can convince me to shake the Lord emotionally and spiritually.

"I was depleted when I came back. Unchristian as some of our actions were over there, no one could get one to give up my faith in Christ. I was a medic and I wanted to give my service to the Lord and people. I'd pray over my wounded and the crew chief would tell the pilot to . . . he would say, 'Be quiet' or 'Shut up!' Because his medic was praying. People were bleeding to death. I'd always pray for the wounded. That was just my reaction. I'd pray out loud. But this is true. It was nothing to fly sixty, seventy days straight.

"In Vietnam one time the zips had come through with grenades and AK-47s and they shot these kids all to pieces. There were little three, four and five, on up to nine and ten year-old kids. They lived in an orphanage and they just shot these kids to pieces.

"We picked them up. And there was this mamasan that had half of her jawbone off and half of her skull exposed here. She was working, she had her hand around a little girl's leg that had been blown off. I started working on her and I was working on this little girl, too, putting a tourniquet on her leg, and I had to get mamasan to let go. She grabbed my hand and I was holding gauze up on her jaw and she was trying to get me to . . . she wanted me to stop working on her and start working on the children. Because she knew that . . . she was gonna die . . . and she didn't want me to waste my time with her. And that's pretty selfless. I saw a lot of selfless things that people did.

"Right now I can look back at a lot of this and I can say civilian life is pretty boring . . . except for the fact that . . . a lot of people ask me, they say, 'You know you were pretty lucky coming back from Vietnam after flying in a Medevac.' I have to tell 'em there wasn't any luck involved. It was by Grace. I just don't believe that there was luck involved in that. I just really believe that the Lord really had his hand on my life, and on the rest of that unit there. He answered my prayers and he answered a lot of other people's prayers who prayed that the Lord would keep everybody safe, and keep them from getting wounded or killed. Nobody in my unit was killed in that whole period of time when there should have been a lot of people killed and a lot of people's lives lost. As far as I'm concerned, it was a miracle that nobody was killed after all the things that we went through. I would just consider that to be Grace and I'm really thankful even today for that.

"It's taken me a long time to go through a lot of things in my life and a lot of people don't understand about Vietnam veterans, that we sacrificed a lot. I feel that a person who flew in the medical . . . or did any type of medical service over there, as far as working with the wounded all the day long, suffered scars that you can't really see on the outside . . . because you have to put a hold on your emotions. As a medic, you can't get emotionally involved with people or their wounds or what they're going through because you wouldn't be able to work on the next person if you did. So I think there's a numbness that sets in and it's a hard thing to overcome later on because that numbness is still there. It is easy to shut off, if you don't want to deal with something. It's easy to shut off and to go into that numbness.

Don's wife: "That automatic shut off was what I ran up against in our relationship when we first met. There was always that wall."

Don: "I think it was a preventive to getting hurt or allowing emotions to get ripped apart. Anyway, I know that now you just take one day at a time.

"I went into a VA hospital for delayed stress. Really, they didn't know too much about delayed stress. They treated it like . . . it was depression that had set in.

"That was at the VA hospital in Vancouver in Oregon. There were a lot of other combat veterans there. A lot of them were there because they had therapy to deal with bitterness and anger and so forth. But basically, I can say after about 1976, I started drinking real hard, I started drinking again. I was drinking a lot trying to forget about the war.

"A lot of other veterans didn't seem to have too much trouble but like I said, working on wounded and having guys die in your arms all the time, it does something to a guy. Seeing all that blood day in and day out. Very little rest. Not eating right. I weighed a hundred and five pounds when I came home. And I was mentally, physically, and spiritually depleted and it eventually took its toll.

"But I don't drink anymore and I don't use drugs and I'm really thankful to God for that and just appreciate Jesus."

Chapter Fourteen

A Dream of Falling Out Backwards

Don Neptune
1970-71
Medevacs

"One of the guys who was in the line--and there was a light rain fallin', it was an overcast day, with that red clay, mud, and the smell, the hot, humid . . . it was hot, but it as a light rain fallin' and one of the guys, who was in the line, said to the MPs, 'OK, today you're gonna die.' He said, 'You're gonna get some of us, but you're gonna die . . . today. So you better think about what that man's tellin' you down there.'"Don Neptune, Medic, U.S. Army

Like a Pariah
Like I Never Left
His Hand is Greater than ...
Surrounded by Trees
A Red Hue to it, Terrifying

Like a Pariah

"A month before I left, I was breaking in a new crew chief . . . flying missions. This was a kind of a difficult period because my crew chief quit flying and went into maintenance, and I was used to flying with him. It was kind of difficult because the person who I was breaking in really didn't have any flight experience. That's how they did it, they took a new guy and just put him in.

"The crew chief's job was to maintain and take care of the ship. On the ship, he operated the hoist, he also was a gunner, and he also helped me work on patients. He would also jump out and run and pick up wounded as I would.

"His relationship to the pilots was that that was *his* helicopter, and he took care of it. That was because they were constantly rotating pilots on the helicopter. It was his helicopter, and he took care of it, he replaced all the instruments that went out, and kept it in flight performance. He was the mechanic. They would take it in, and every twenty-five hours they would perform a PM (Preventive Maintenance) on it, and then every three-hundred hours they would . . . Other people did it with him, other maintenance people who didn't fly but were strictly maintenance. Other crew chiefs *did* work on their helicopters when they would come into maintenance, but they were back in the rear. They weren't out in the field flying missions at some firebase or whatnot.

"I think my crew chief, Darrel, was eighteen. I was twenty. He was very mature for his age. I flew with him startin' about in October, the latter part of October, clear up until June, maybe the end of June or July.

"Before I left I was breaking in a new crew chief because Darrel was gettin' short and he was goin' to go into maintenance. We'd had three engine failures on the helicopter, and he was takin' a lot of heat. It was an old bird.

"I think I flew with my crew chief up into July and I broke in this guy in August. I quit flying about a week and a half before leaving. The new guy was young, he was young, too. His name was Batten, and he was from Montana. He wanted to fly really bad, but the CO, our Commanding Officer, told me he wasn't ready, he wasn't ready to fly. He just wasn't ready for it. Finally, he was there about four or five months and they let him fly. Well, at that time they needed a crew chief and he was available to fly; since it was a volunteer basis type of deal, he had volunteered. Other people didn't want to volunteer to fly. They quit or ended their tour.

"So the last thirty days I was training this new guy in the rudiments of patient pickups, and how to work with Vietnamese radio men; sometimes when we'd fly we'd pick up a Vietnamese radio man. I taught him how to work with the Vietnamese radio man, and how to coordinate the LZ (landing zone) in the pickup. We would take a radio man up with us and he would contact people on the ground. He had the same kind of radio as the guys on the ground. I think he had a PRIC 25 (known as a Prick 25). Also, we flew South Korean missions. We would take a South Korean medic along with us. Not a radio man, but he would have a radio with him.

"The radio man dealt with codes. We'd just coordinate the pickup, and made sure this was the right area of operations where we were goin' in. The pilot would ask for a certain type of smoke, and I would tell the radio man to tell the people on the ground to pop that color.

"I don't believe we came under any fire during those last thirty days when I was breaking in the new guy. If we did, it's just like so many missions that I flew, we coulda been taking fire and not even really known it, because we usually had gunship support.

"I was starting to get more nervous as I got ready to go home. But in fact, I helped to break in two crew chiefs. Another guy's name was Webster and he went to fly on another helicopter, but I did fly missions with him. So there were two crew chiefs that were breaking in, learning how to fly.

"I didn't go to Vietnam until 1970, so I saw a lot of the anti-war demonstrations before I went over there. I didn't agree with their sentiments. When I got back to Seattle I wore my uniform, and it was bad. At the time I got to the terminal, I was gonna catch a flight back to the Tri-Cities but it was pretty radical, and there was a lot of people, kind of hippie-like . . . that was 1971 . . . it was kind of strange . . . these kind of people wore really long hair . . . and wore Army trench coats and jackets with sergeant stripes on 'em, and they were really radical, I remember being slandered in that airport by them, things said, you know, 'Baby killer' and whatnot. I was on my way home. And I remember I went and sat down. I went to the bus terminal to catch a bus and I sat down on a bench where the other people were sitting down on the bench . . . and everybody got off the bench when I sat down on the bench. They got up and moved off the bench. They walked about ten feet away from me and turned around and looked at me, just stared at me while I was waitin' for my bus. No one would talk to me or anything like that. It was quite strange. I felt very like a pariah.

"But I remember the bus driver said he appreciated me . . . serving my country. I hadn't expected that, what these other people had said. The comin' back, the first three days, I had some friends, and they threw a party for me. It was over in Kennewick. They were out of high school, living in Kennewick; they were working, high school guys, a lot of them were going to college during that time. It was right before college started back up again. I remember there were several of 'em at this party and I had a lot of people asking me some strange questions. There were others there who were defending me. It kinda made me feel like people were talkin' about me like I'm not even there. But yet they're talking about me in my presence. It was kind of an intimidating situation.

"And I remember somebody asking me if we were winning the war, and another guy who wasn't a Vietnam veteran, he told the guy, 'Well, do you have a nickel in your pocket?' And the guy said, 'Yeah.' And he said, 'Well, flip the coin and lick a side.' It was just kinda . . . you know, at that time it was basically the way these people were.

"I really couldn't communicate with them. I felt a lot more mature . . . about life and things. It was easier for me to communicate with an older person than those people of my own age or peer group.

"I remember at that party that they shut off the lights and threw a firecracker in my face. I flipped over in the chair and I was just shaking. They turned back on the lights and I said, 'Why?'.

"And they said, 'Well, we just wanted to see if what they said was real about Vietnam.' And I left that party and I've never seen them since."

Like I Never Left

"I was still in the service, I had eighteen months to go. I went down to Fort Stewart, Georgia, and I went into a company, a helicopter unit called the 498th. It was a Medevac unit, but it was not established. We didn't have any helicopters. We had a commanding officer, and that was it. He came around once a month and he gave us our payroll checks. The rest of the time we sat there, and we sat there for about *six* months doing nothing. All these Vietnam veterans.

"We didn't have a tv there, and then later on we got a tv. But tv didn't interest me. The town was Hanesville, Georgia. This was a military town, and there were a lot of veterans who lived in Hanesville, retired veterans. It's a small community, a rural farming area.

"In a small town like that you are never treated like we had been treated in Seattle or other big cities. But we were basically ignored. In most military towns, you're ignored by the populace. Other than when you go off . . . But I just really didn't feel comfortable being out in the town. I couldn't stand being around a lot of people. The other veterans were all basically the same way . . . nervous, kind of. We didn't discuss things, not too much. We played cards. We didn't talk much about the war. It was kind of like . . . we were still in the war. I remember talking, speaking the same type of lingo that we spoke over in Vietnam back in the states up to a year after we got back. Because all I was around was Vietnam veterans. And then they brought in a bunch of guys who were brand new out of AIT, and they were medics, and crew chief maintenance people to work on helicopters. And then they brought in our helicopters and we started flying missions supporting civilian traffic. Accidents, and flying patients from hospital to hospital. And also we were picking up patients who were coming back from Vietnam on the planes. Most of these were drug rehab patients because they had a drug rehab center at Fort Stewart. Really hard core heroin addicts from Vietnam. They had come straight from either the 6th CC which was a major heroin ... it was kind of like a little prison there that they had.

"They had a guard on board. On all those flights, they had MPs on board. But these guys were on amnesty programs, so they brought 'em in, but most of them were given dishonorable discharges eventually. Most of these guys were white . . . there was some bloods (African Americans) there.

"It was kind of a shock to go on board those military flights with wounded guys back from Vietnam; they were flying them to another hospital. And I'd come on the plane and it would smell just like Vietnam. It was instant. It would be like I never left. You know coming back on that plane, picking up those guys, I thought to myself, 'I thought I was over with this, and here I'm not.'

"All these guys were pretty badly wounded. These guys had the NG tubes and the nasal tubes and the IVs. Pretty bad shape, these guys were.

"I remember at Hunter Army Air Field, which was at Savannah, we had friends. I knew some guys who had flown on gunships, who had come back from Vietnam. They had flown in a gunship company that used to support our unit. I knew one guy and he got killed out on the tarmac. He walked out, right into the tail rotor blade. I think he committed suicide. He was really having some bad problems. He had been shot down about twelve times. He flew in Loaches, on those hunter-killer teams that would go in and draw fire. The cobras would be circling about six-thousand feet and they would come down after they drew fire. Then they would back off and tell them where the enemy was, and blast 'em.

"Since I've come back, I've tried to get away from calling the enemy the slang terms that we used over in Vietnam--gooks, slopes, zips, all that. Not that it means anything for the enemy, but I always felt that it was derogatory.

"After I left the 12th Evac Hospital and started flying, I thought I had seen quite a bit of working on wounded, but really, after I started flying I realized that I hadn't seen anything. And after about two weeks you get pretty cold real quick. You can't get emotionally involved with people that you're working on or you'll go crazy. You won't be able to work on the next person that comes along, or you won't be able to function and do your job. There's a numbness that sets in that's quite devastating because you're not able to let your emotions out normally or naturally. What takes place is that you're not able to shut off your emotions or turn them on at will.

"As far as my beliefs were concerned, I still had compassion for the wounded and I prayed continuously for them, for my unit. But it was amazing for me to watch guys come in out of the field who'd been flying missions, because the first thing that they would do would be to get high, to get drunk, to get loaded to just . . . to get away from that. Also it was kinda like if you hadn't taken fire, you were a cherry boy. You know, you hadn't been there yet. If you hadn't taken fire, if you hadn't been shot at, or shot, you were still cherry, you were still a virgin--you didn't know what was really going on.

"And I remember my first week, when we were flying and when I was being trained, the guy that was training me was named Charlie Martinez. And I don't know if I told you about how he pulled the armor plating back from the pilot when we were taking fire on a mission. And the pilot was screaming 'Put my armor plate back!'

"And he said, 'I only have seventeen days left. You ain't gettin' no armor plate.' And he was up behind it. And the pilot kept on screaming for him to push his armor plating back up and he wasn't gonna do it. This was when I first started flying, he was training me. And the pilot said, 'What if I get hit?'

"And he said, 'I'll jerk you outta there and fly this baby back to the states!' I thought that was kinda funny and . . . it was . . . but really, the pilot was a pretty new pilot, and Charlie said, 'You ain't been here long enough, nuke, to warrant this armor plating!' He said that to the pilot. "Ha!' he said, 'You ain't been here long enough to warrant this armor plating.'

"And here I am, sitting there, and I didn't have any armor plating. But I had a chicken plate on, I remember I had a chicken plate. And that's twenty pounds of lead in front and back. But it kind of gave *me* a *fear* because of . . . hey, these guys are really shootin' at us! Tryin' to shoot us down. Of course, that wouldn't have been classified as the real thing. I would still have been classified as a cherry or a virgin because I wasn't the medic on board by myself as being a medic, being under that type of circumstance. But yeah, we was flyin' to an LZ (landing zone) and they said we were taking fire. He pulled the armor plating back.

"I had been around pretty hard type people before I went over to Vietnam. But when I got over there, it was totally different. We were on call . . . and not eating right . . . and the war was continually there. You were always on, you had to be. It wasn't even a point of motivation. It wasn't even to get the job done. It was to the point like 'We got a mission. We gotta go fly a mission. We gotta go pick up wounded, or we get a call in by radio man . . . go! That's it! Just run out to your helicopter, and get on and go!'

"I remember being in the hospital at Cu Chi. How it was so strange. You couldn't even call Cu Chi the rear . . . but it *was*. I mean we were safe at Cu Chi, basically. I remember there was some perimeter fighting at certain times but we weren't near any of that what was going on.

"I think I told you the story about the guys who came in from the field who were standing in line waitin' to go into the PX. These guys, was maybe fifty, sixty guys. And they were standing in line waiting to go into the PX. These guys had just come right out of the field. They had their rucksacks on, they had their machine guns, machetes and knives hanging off of them. Sawed-off shotguns and M-60s, the whole ball of wax. And there was a colonel up at the door who was dressed in brand new fatigues, brand new jungle boots, baseball cap, and all these guys had boonie hats on, and their hair was considerably long, they had pony tails, some of them did.

"They were 9th Infantry troops, and the colonel had a barber set up there to give them a haircut and a shave and he wanted them to get their boots shined. And these guys were going right back out in the field in two or three days. And they didn't want a haircut, and they didn't want their shoes shined. They just wanted to go into the PX. There was a big argument going on. The colonel was by himself but there was a couple lieutenants there also dressed up like the colonel. I remember these 9th Infantry guys standing in line, and then this colonel got on the radio and he called in two jeeploads of MPs. And the MPs came in there and they locked and loaded their M-60s on these guys who were in line. That's how tense it got.

"One of the guys who was in the line--and there was a light rain fallin', it was an overcast day, with that red clay, mud, and the smell, the hot, humid . . . it was *hot*, but it as a light rain fallin' and one of the guys, who was in the line, said to the MPs, 'OK, today you're gonna die.' He said, 'You're gonna get some of us, but you're gonna die . . . today. So you better think about what that man's tellin' you down there.'

"And all these guys all at once started pulling off their machine guns, and whipping up their M-60s and breakin' out their shotguns and their M-16s, and I seen some AK-47s also. And all of a sudden there was a showdown between the MPs in the jeep and these guys standin' in line weapons pointing. And the guys in the jeeps, the MPs, were gettin' really scared, and they kept on looking back over at this colonel and back at these guys, and finally they kicked their barrels of their M-60s, back up in the air.

"The colonel didn't tell the MPs to kick their M-60s back up, they just did it. I just left because the argument was continuing, they weren't gettin' anywhere. I think finally they just let 'em go in. Yeah, they just let 'em go in. That's what happened, the colonel and his lieutenants eventually just backed out of the way.

"I was standin' there watchin' all of this goin' down."

His Hand is Greater Than ...

"I had a friend who was in several situations where they refused to go out in the field. He was a point man for ten months at Chu Lai before he stepped on a land mine. He lives around here, Kennewick. He goes up in Alaska, he fishes, he's got a boat.

"He supports himself but he draws the disability. His name's Joe. He almost lost his leg. He had taken off his helmet, was carrying it underneath his arm when he stepped on the mine. He said normally they wore boonie hats but at that time they were wearing their steel pots. It saved him from gettin' his arm blown off and losing his eyes. But he still spent six months in Japan in the hospital. He about died. He was blown twelve feet in the air and he came down and he was in a mud puddle. And he could see himself--he was hovering above his body and he could see himself lying there. He was saying 'I'm gonna die. I'm gonna die.' And he heard a voice say, 'No, you're not.' They medevaced him out and the medic in the helicopter saved his life because the medic on the ground hadn't found a piece of shrapnel that had cut his femoral artery. The medic on the helicopter clamped it off. But he's got scars that run up and down his body that look just like razor blades that just sliced him open. The meat had just been rolled back. All up and down his whole body. But he lived. I saw him right before I went over to Vietnam. He came in to our church. He was on crutches. I was just gettin' ready to go. He showed me some pictures.

"I had a dream before I went over to Vietnam that I was going to be flying a helicopter. I had a dream that I fell out of the helicopter. It was in a jungle; it was like a fully living-color movie, a panorama. This *dream* I had! I could hear the rotor blades, the whop! whop! I'd forgotten about that whole dream when I went over to Vietnam.

"I had a dream that I was in a helicopter, and there was a jungle, and that I fell out. I dreamt I was falling out backwards, but I never hit the ground. I could see the jungle below, the triple canopy. But when I went over there I started working in a hospital and forgot all about that dream. Then when I volunteered for Dustoff, I had to remember that dream. When I got on that helicopter, I remembered. As we were flying off, I remembered that dream, and I said, 'Oh, no!'

"But really, being a Christian, I felt that maybe that was from the Lord. That the Lord had shown me something, and to be careful. My crew chief almost fell out of the helicopter one time. He almost walked right out, right out of it. And I warned him. He felt that maybe it had something to do with it. It could also be that while I was over there . . . that the dream showed me that God's Grace is everlasting. I believe that you can fall from His grace, but *His* grace is everlasting. If we turn back to Him, He is *still* here willing to take us back in. So maybe I felt that this was kind of showing me a little bit about my Christian walk as far as my relationship with Christ. I don't know, I never hit the ground. I think His hand is greater than . . . But just to go on a dream like that . . .

"When I was stationed at Fort Stewart, we used to fly to Augusta. We used to fly to Charleston, South Carolina, and we used to fly along the coast there and over the Okefenokee Swamp, and we'd fly all over Georgia. The Swamp used to remind me of Vietnam. It was quiet. It was quiet. But we did get shot at over Savannah one night. There were tracer rounds, and what was funny about it was that my captain was a Vietnam veteran, an AC, which is aircraft commander. He flew on the left hand side up front. The guy to his right is the co-pilot, fresh out of Fort Rucker flight school. The crew chief was not a Vietnam veteran either. And I asked the captain, the pilot, 'Could you go up private for a minute?'

"He said, 'Sure.'

"I said, 'Did you see what I saw?' You can go up on the radio private because otherwise you'll key the mike and everybody can hear what you're saying. See, we kinda didn't wanna say anything because . . .

"He said, 'Well, what did you see?'

"I said, 'I saw tracers.'

"He said, 'That's what I *saw*.'

"I said, 'Don't you think you better take some evasive action?'

"He said, 'Taking evasive action, right now.' And he buzzed off. When you take evasive action in a helicopter, you kind of do a roll, a pitchout. You don't roll the helicopter, you just kind of roll out. Take a different heading, you might drop or gain altitude, depending. You usually drop altitude.

"But we were flying, probably at six-thousand feet. We were near Savannah. We never did tell the other two guys about it. Never did. They didn't even know what it was. They didn't even realize it. I remember the co-pilot saying, 'What was that?' But the aircraft commander didn't say anything."

"It could've been a veteran down there. Most of the guys in our unit were pretty hostile to the military after coming back from Vietnam. We couldn't identify with stateside duty--at all. We were just saying, 'Why don't they just let us out? We can't finish our tours. I could have extended while I was over there to get an early out but I really felt glad to leave. It was a high pressure situation. A lot of guys did extend their tours to get out early, but they were crew chiefs who could go into maintenance and didn't have to fly. As a medic, I didn't have that option. I would have had to continue to fly missions. I remember I did get scared one night . . . and I got *sick*. I don't know, I think I just got sick from fear one night.

"We had had this Green Beret come into our unit as a medic. He had volunteered to fly Dustoff. I don't know why he didn't stay with his unit. He didn't talk about it. His name was Clyde. He came in, he was a little bit older than me. He had just started flying missions, he was breakin' in, and he was flyin' in his own bird. Well, he had taken over a bird, and he was a good medic, but really didn't have a lot of flight time. I think fear gripped me so bad that night that he took that mission. I had another medic threaten me that if I ever did that again . . . I *froze up*. That was late in my tour, right before I was gonna come home. I got cold feet, sad to say. But he flew that mission for me, and the other medic, his name was Sanders, he snapped me back to reality. He didn't hit me or anything, but he talked to me real harsh-like. Told me never to do that again, and I didn't."

Surrounded by Trees

"I remember when we were flying missions, we'd call the pilots 'cowboys.' (I don't know if you've ever heard that term before.) These Dustoff pilots are probably some of your *best* pilots flying helicopters. I'm serious. These guys could land on a dime. Normally, we didn't ever land, we just hovered there to pick up the wounded, but it's just the terminology. But they could be flyin' a hundred and forty knots and come in low-level and fly through that triple-canopy jungle and just weave through that stuff. I've been surrounded by trees flying through the jungle, it's just amazing what those guys can do. Just excellent pilots! No fear whatsoever. Just talkin' and carryin' on a conversation just like nothin' was goin' on.

"If we started taking fire or if there were presumed enemy positions, they would call in gunships. If we had 'em available. A lot of times we didn't have gunships available, but we'd still fly the mission. Generally, the gunships would be following us flying patient protection. The gunships would be flyin' up in the mountains, and a lot of 'em would have to shoot off half their load of ammo because they were so heavily weighted down. When we'd get up in the mountains, it'd be five, six thousand feet among those big pine trees. Beautiful. I remember a lot of 'em having to turn around and go back. Couldn't make it. Sometimes we'd call in 'Spooky.' They'd call in a gunship or they'd call in 'Puff the Magic Dragon.' We'd just be flyin' around waitin' to go in and land after he'd do his run. We'd pick up the wounded.

"Spooky's fire would be like a straight red line, criss-crossing, and arcing and so forth. I saw green tracers, the same. The enemy used green tracers a lot. I remember a tracer coming right for my face one time. We were flyin', movin', and it was coming right for my face, and it just veered off. It was really close. It was so close I could almost feel the heat; it just went away from me.

A Red Hue to It

"Back in the states I didn't really enjoy flying. In fact, I was given an option because when I came back to the states I wasn't ready to go back in the service. I stayed out an extra two weeks, so basically I was AWOL (Absent Without Leave). I remember going back and my CO sat down and talked to me. He said, 'Look, we're gonna establish a Medevac unit here.'

"And I said, 'I don't wanna fly anymore.'

"He said, 'Look, you're two weeks AWOL. You don't have much of a choice. Either you fly or you go to the stockade.' He was a Vietnam veteran. He had been a pilot over there. He was a Medevac pilot, so I knew he was a good pilot.

"I didn't want to go to the stockade, I couldn't handle that. So I told 'im I'd fly. So they made me senior flight medic.

"We had two medics who came in from Vietnam that were infantry medics, and the CO made me the senior flight medic even though they outranked me. He did this because I had flown Dustoff. One guy was pretty irritated about it, but yet he didn't have any air time. He wasn't a flight medic. So it's a big difference as far as your flight medics and your ground medics. I will say your flight medics have more to work with. I'm not trying to make the infantry medic look bad but the flight medic was continually exposed to wounded people. Continually working on eight, nine guys, five, six all the time, all day long. You go into an LZ, you pick up two or three or four or five or whatever. You don't usually pick up one; you're picking up several at a time in one LZ, and maybe making several runs back to pick up more wounded out of that same LZ, and either flying them to a hospital or you've got another medevac who'd meet you half way because you can't leave that AO (area of operations); you're continually flying from there for maybe two or three weeks, up to a month or longer.

"I was stateside for another eighteen months. I was on a three-year tour and I pulled every day of it. It was incredibly long. I remember guys driving cars. I finally bought a car in '72. It was really strange to drive again. I started going to church pretty regularly there at Fort Stewart. In fact I was teaching a Bible class to civilians. Most of these kids were Army brats. I was the teacher. Some Air Force personnel attended; one was a lieutenant. I was teaching the Bible.

"I was just teaching Christian . . . Full Gospel. I'm a Full Gospel. I was just teaching the Bible. I believe in the Full Gospel. Some of them went to Baptist churches, some came from all different types of Christian backgrounds. But I don't really know if they had heard the Bible as Jesus taught it, and as the Apostles taught it. It was different, it was new to them. I had felt a lot of pressure doing that and seeking the Lord's will in that. There was quite a few Vietnam veterans who I had shared the Gospel with who became Christians.

"There wasn't a lot to do at Fort Stewart. Some people went to Savannah to go to the ocean, to the beach. There was a problem with drugs in our unit, also. Coming back from Vietnam.

Editor's Note: The interviewer asks if GIs were extracting their own blood to mix with drugs.

Don Neptune Replies: "They were doing it with tuinals and barbiturates; they didn't have a lot of access to heroin. They would take this stuff and crush it down and mix it with water. They'd draw some blood out and mix it with their blood and then shoot it back up into their veins. But most of these guys were into downers. They just scored 'em right there on post. I didn't see too much cocaine, just barbiturates, reds, seconal. That's what reds are, seconal. Most people picked up the heroin habit in Vietnam. They were doing it over there. But they weren't shootin' it over there. Very few of them were shootin' it. Most of them were snortin' it or smoking it. To smoke it, they'd unroll a little bit of tobacco and they'd suck up the heroin with the cigarette. Like inhale it up; they'd knock a little off into a cap and inhale it up into the cigarette, then twist it and shake it down, and then fire it up and smoke it. They'd call these cigarettes CJs because in Vietnam the mamasans who sold it called it cocaine but it wasn't cocaine. It was heroin. I smoked a little bit of it over there but I didn't particularly care for it.

"Of course being a medic, the only way to take drugs if you're goin' to do it is to *inject* it. There was some opium, and we used to sit around and drink coffee with opium mixed in it. We did this in the states, down at Fort Stewart, Georgia.

"We smoke opium, and we mixed it in coffee. It's very bitter. Over in Vietnam, we ate benzedrine . . . to fly, to keep goin'. It's a speed. We also took Ritalin. That's called a mood elevator. It keeps you awake. It was in a liquid form and pills, too. There was also some French stuff that was goin' around through units. It came in little drams.

"Yes, officers took it too. There was no rank involved in that. I caught a pilot snortin' heroin one night before we went on a mission. And I said, 'You're not flyin'.

"The French stuff came in little drams of about 50cc's. You'd mix it in a soft drink and drink it, and it was a speed.

"But the night I stopped, we had heated up some opium, and we injected it. It was melted, it was heated and bubbling, hot, hot. Opium is like black tar. This was Asian.

"You know, the joints (marijuana) didn't have anything in it in Vietnam. It was pure. Some of that was even tested over there. It was not mixed with anything; it was just *that potent*. 'Cause I always thought it was mixed, too, but it wasn't. But they used to lace it, or it was the way they manufactured it, let it dry. The way they cured it, it was cured differently; they used different things to bring out the potency. But most of it, no. It wasn't. Oh, yeah! They called 'em OJs. But that was basically when I was back in the rear. When we weren't flyin', that's basically when I smoked. We called 'em OJs. They'd say 'Opium-cured.'

"So this opium was black tar and it was melted and injected. It about killed me. I about died. I collapsed. I couldn't breathe. I saw red. I saw red. Everything was red. Had a red hue to it. It was not a good feeling. It was terrifying. I felt like my brain was bubbling up. I could hear a 'pop, pop, pop' going across the top of my head. It was very . . . was askin' the Lord right there to help me. This experience probably lasted several hours. At that point, where I was near death . . . I don't know -- because you're in such a weird state of mind . . .

"Then I quit ... in late '75 . . . our relationship had failed, that I had with this ... woman. And I really didn't know which direction I was going in; I felt very alone. My faith was at an all-time low."

- end -